CAREER AND VOCATIONAL EDUCATION FOR MILDLY LEARNING HANDICAPPED AND DISADVANTAGED YOUTH

CAREER AND VOCATIONAL EDUCATION FOR MILDLY LEARNING HANDICAPPED AND DISADVANTAGED YOUTH

By

DAVID C. GARDNER

GRACE JOELY BEATTY

PAULA L. GARDNER

CHARLES C THOMAS • PUBLISHER
Springfield • Illinois • U.S.A.

Published and Distributed Throughout the World by

CHARLES C THOMAS • PUBLISHER
2600 South First Street
Springfield, Illinois 62717

ISBN 0-398-04818-5

Library of Congress Catalog Card Number:

With THOMAS BOOKS *careful attention is given to all details of manufacturing and design. It is the Publisher's desire to present books that are satisfactory as to their physical qualities and artistic possibilities and appropriate for their particular use.* THOMAS BOOKS *will be true to those laws of quality that assure a good name and good will.*

Printed in the United States of America
Q-R-1

Library of Congress Cataloging in Publication Data

Gardner, David C.
Career and vocational education for mildly learning handicapped and disadvantaged youth.
Bibliography: p.
Includes index.
1. Learning disabilities. 2. Socially handicapped youth — Education. 3. Mentally handicapped youth — Vocational education. 4. Career education. 5. Vocational education. I. Beatty, Grace Joely. II. Gardner, Paula L. III. Title.
LC4704.G37 1984 371.92'82 83-640
ISBN 0-398-04818-5

BIOGRAPHICAL SKETCHES

Dr. David C. Gardner is a licensed psychologist, an associate professor at Boston University, and co-founder of American Training and Research Associates, Inc. He was director of several large federally funded projects on vocational training for handicapped persons. He is a past president of the National Association for Career Education and a founding officer and former board member of the Eastern Educational Research Association. Dr. Gardner is a member of the National Ethics Committee of the American Association on Mental Deficiency and was recently nominated for vice president of the Vocational Rehabilitation Division. He is a member of the Research Committee, Division of Career Development, Council for Exceptional Children. He recently received the Professional Award, American Association on Mental Deficiency, Region X. He is listed in *Who's Who in the East,* a companion volume to Marquis's *Who's Who in America,* 1981, and was a member of the Board of Directors, New England Securities Depository Trust Company of the Boston Stock Exchange.

Dr. Gardner earned his master's and doctorate in educational psychology (special education) at Boston University and a Bachelor of Arts from Northeastern University. Dr. Gardner has received a number of honors including Certificates of Recognition from the State Board of Education, Illinois Office of Education (1975); the U.S. Office of Education, Office of Career Education (1976); and the National Association for Career Education (1979).

Dr. Gardner is a frequent speaker at national and regional professional meetings and workshops and has appeared on radio and television. He has authored/co-authored over 100 publications. His recent books are *Career and Disabilities* (1978); *Dissertation Proposal Guidebook: How to Prepare a Research Proposal and Get it Accepted* (1980); *How to Plan Training Programs* (1981); and *Career and Vocational*

Education for the Handicapped and Disadvantaged (1983). Dr. Gardner was editor of *Career Education Quarterly* (1975-80) and a consulting editor of *Mental Retardation* (1972-77). He is currently a member of the editorial board of *College Student Journal* and a consulting editor of *Career Development for Exceptional Individuals.*

Dr. Grace Joely Beatty is co-founder of American Training and Research Associates, Inc. Dr. Beatty earned her doctoral degree in career development education from Boston University, a Master of Education in business from Boston University, and a Bachelor of Arts in business administration from Simmons College. In addition, she recently completed a postdoctoral audit in research and evaluation through the Eastern Educational Research Association.

Dr. Beatty recently served as project director of a major federal research grant on the handicapped. She previously served as associate director of a federally funded research project on training entry-level workers to master technical language. She was a senior research associate and visiting lecturer at Boston University for several years. Dr. Beatty has had extensive experience in training students from diverse economic backgrounds for positions in business and industry. She is an expert in computer analysis of research data and is in demand as a consultant to both educational and industrial organizations.

Dr. Beatty has received a number of honors. She was awarded a federal stipend for her doctoral studies and recently received a Certificate of Recognition from the National Association for Career Education. She was elected to two honorary scholarly societies, Phi Delta Kappa and Delta Pi Epsilon, during her graduate studies. She has held a number of offices in national and regional professional organizations. Dr. Beatty was elected an "Outstanding Young Woman of America" in 1978.

Dr. Beatty is a frequent speaker at regional and national professional meetings and workshops. She has appeared on local radio and has authored/co-authored over thirty professional publications. These include journal articles, editorials, monographs, curriculum guides, and training manuals. Her most recent books are *Dissertation Proposal Guidebook: How to Prepare a Research Proposal and Get it Accepted* (1980); *How to Plan Training Programs* (1981); and *Career and Vocational Education for the Handicapped and Disadvantaged* (1983). Dr. Beatty was special issues editor, *Career Education Quarterly.*

Dr. Paula L. Gardner is a licensed special agent for the New York Life Insurance Company specializing in estate planning for families of handicapped persons. She is also a senior consultant with American Training and Research Associates, Inc., responsible for developing training programs to help teachers become more effective. She was an adjunct lecturer in special education and career education at Boston University from 1972 to 1980. Dr. Gardner specialized in methods of teaching the handicapped and developed a course on adapting vocational and business curricula for special populations. She has taught "normal" adults and elementary students as well as various handicapped students, including mentally retarded, learning disabled, emotionally disturbed, and physically handicapped persons. She is a former teacher-coordinator of a special needs vocational high school program and has worked as a cooperative education program supervisor and as a placement specialist. She has taught in adult education programs and coordinated Title I summer programs with disadvantaged children, which included planning an elementary (K-8) career education curriculum. In addition, Dr. Gardner has had many years of experience in programming for the mainstreaming of special needs students at the elementary and secondary levels.

Dr. Gardner received the Bachelor of Science degree in elementary education, the Master of Education degree in special education, and the Doctor of Education degree in human development from Boston University. She has worked as a consultant on numerous federal, state, and locally funded projects for mentally retarded and handicapped students. She is the author or co-author of numerous publications, which include articles in national professional journals, curriculum guides, grant reports, and editorials. In addition to serving as associate editor of *Career Education Quarterly* (1974-80), Dr. Gardner served as consulting editor for *Mental Retardation* (1974-77). She is a frequent speaker at national and regional meetings and is in great demand as a workshop leader and teaching specialist for in-service programs and projects. Dr. Gardner is listed in "Outstanding Young Women in America" (1980).

ACKNOWLEDGMENTS

WE wish to acknowledge the support of all our colleagues and students who have provided us with those critical insights so necessary to the development of a work such as this one. In particular we wish to thank Dr. Elizabeth A. Bigelow, Dr. Kevin Dwyer, and Dr. Kenneth G. Webber for their reading of and helpful comments on the manuscript.

D.C.G.
G.J.B.
P.L.G.

CONTENTS

CAREER AND VOCATIONAL EDUCATION FOR MILDLY LEARNING HANDICAPPED AND DISADVANTAGED YOUTH

CHAPTER 1

INTRODUCTION

SCOTT came from an impoverished and broken home. His father left when Scott was an infant and shortly thereafter divorced his mother. All through his childhood and during his formative teenage years, Scott was without a male role model at home. When he entered high school, he did so as a member of the first "special class" of high school aged students in the history of his community. Previously, special class services ended with junior high school. Scott read at the third grade level upon entering high school and handled mathematics at about the ninth grade level. He had been labeled "mentally retarded" by the school system.

Until he joined the work study program, Scott was withdrawn in school and had no friends. His involvement in this program added immensely to his overall education, and four years later Scott graduated with a high school diploma. Seven years after entering the program, Scott had a good job as a night manager in a service station, his own car, an apartment, and a circle of friends. Scott was a contributing member of society and was, in fact, no longer "retarded."

During this period of phenomenal personal and career growth for Scott, there were many changes in the legislation and attitudes of educators and society in general about what constituted an appropriate education for students like Scott. No longer could children be isolated in "special classes" without an extensive evaluation and due process. No longer could children like Scott be denied an equal opportunity for a "normal" education and a high school diploma. Moreover, during this period, legislation and changes in attitudes about the need for career and vocational education for all youth made an impact on the curriculum of most public school systems in the country. Thus, children like Scott were given appropriate support services, instruction, and opportunities to reach their full potential and become active participating members of our society.

This book is written for teachers, counselors, parents, and other persons who want to work with children like Scott (or "Mary") and whose goals are the same as ours: to find ways to break down the many barriers to successful employment and life adjustment for youth like the Scotts of this world.

This book is entitled *Career and Vocational Education for Mildly Learning Handicapped and Disadvantaged Youth.* What we mean by these terms will be explained in more detail in the definitions section of this chapter. We are calling attention to the title here to make a point about Scott and others like him. If we were to examine Scott's records today, in the context of the new laws and definitions of handicapped or disadvantaged, it would be difficult to label Scott. We could make equally cogent cases for labeling Scott as learning disabled or as economically disadvantaged. The point is that the label is not important (except insofar as it is important to the school administration for obtaining funding to provide services for Scott). What is important is the kind of programs and support services that are made available to Scott.

All of us interested in career/vocational education for special populations are aware of the phenomenal growth in the number of programs and laws about such programs since the early 1960s. The laws on vocational education, career education, and the education of handicapped and disadvantaged youth in general have helped make impressive gains in the number and quality of programs and services for these two populations. Moreover, the federal government has mandated these areas as "high priority" for funding in an attempt to broaden the knowledge and programs available. Countless monies have been allocated to research, program development, and vocational and career education for handicapped and disadvantaged persons of all ages. Yet, if one were to ask the practitioner in the field about the state of the art, undoubtedly the answer would be "We have a long way to go."

For most readers, a discussion of definitions can be dry, especially if you think of them as simply words on a piece of paper to be memorized (or ignored). Yet definitions determine the thrust of organizational efforts — they are particularly important to the federal government's endeavors, to state departments of education, and to other human service agencies. Funding and programs are ultimately tied to definitions contained in legislation and agency regulations. Moreover, most definitions represent the consensus of the people who have organized themselves to achieve a specific set of objectives. Knowledge of the terms they agree upon yields a better understanding of their objectives and strategies. Finally, unless you have an understanding of what we mean by the key terms in this text, you may not be conceptualizing on the same plane we are. For example, if you think of "fruit" as being apples and oranges and we think of "fruit" as being grapes, bananas, and pears, we are talking about very different things, even though we are using the same word.

DEFINITION OF CAREER/VOCATIONAL EDUCATION FOR HANDICAPPED AND DISADVANTAGED

There are some key words and phrases used throughout this book that should be studied before reading the chapters that follow. These terms are *career education, vocational education, mildly learning handicapped,* and *disadvantaged.* This next section presents an overview of the common definitions of these terms and provides a framework for understanding what we mean by them in this book.

Most textbook authors agree that there is no universally accepted definition of *career education* (e.g. Brolin & Kokaska, 1979; Clark, 1979; Gardner & Warren, 1978). That there is no universally accepted definition is consistent with the philosophy of Sidney Marland, Jr. (1974), the former assistant secretary of education who initiated the career education movement in the Office of Education. Marland felt that the definition of *career education* should be left to the individual practitioners in the schools. In principle we agree with Marland, but the practical reality is that to fund programs in career education, the government needs to be able to specify what it means when it funds a particular program.

There are several often quoted definitions of *career education.* Probably the most frequently cited one appears in the book written by Hoyt, Evans, Mackin, and Mangum (1974):

> Career education is the total effort of public education and the community to help all individuals become familiar with the values of a work-oriented society, to integrate these values into their personal value systems, and to implement these values in their lives in such a way that work becomes possible, meaningful, and satisfying to each individual.

(Hoyt et al., 1974, p. 15)

In a later document published by the U.S. Office of Education as a policy paper, Hoyt (1975) defines *career education* as "the totality of experiences through which one learns about, and prepares to engage in, work as part of his or her way of living" (p. 4). Both of the above are rather broad definitions of training for work when compared to the more narrow definition of vocational education to be discussed later. However, Clark (1979) views these two definitions of *career education* as *too narrow,* suggesting that they are an attempt to "restore the credibility of the Protestant work ethic. . ." (Clark, 1979, p. 5). He feels that they definitely reflect bias toward a person's economic life or paid work (Clark, 1979, p. 5). Within the context of career education for the handicapped, Clark (1979) and Brolin & Kokaska (1979) take a much broader view of the term by emphasizing the process of preparing for life, rather than just preparation for making a living. As will be seen later, we tend to agree with Brolin, Kokaska, and Clark in that we also believe in a broader definition, the difference being that we include vocational education in our broader definition.

As with *career education,* the term *vocational education* is defined in varying ways. Here is a summary of the most frequently used definitions:

> Vocational education has been conceptualized as secondary education, focused on training persons for gainful employment in recognized occupations in skilled or semi-skilled positions. (Gardner, 1978, p. 801)

Since we are proposing a new definition that is a synthesis of career education and vocational education, it might be helpful to the reader if we take a moment to talk about the philosophical differences between career educators and vocational educators. Most practitioners who call themselves career educators would point to their concern about providing skills for children of *all* ages that will help to prepare them for life in a work-oriented society. The focus of career education is on general work skills, such as attitudes, job search skills, interpersonal skills, work habits such as neatness, etc. Career education begins in kindergarten and provides services and training throughout a person's productive life, even into retirement.

Vocational educators, on the other hand, would characterize their interest as one that deals with secondary and postsecondary persons and with preparing these individuals for a specific paid occupation, e.g. plumber, carpenter, etc. Figure 1 provides a list of differences in focus and philosophy between vocational and career educators. It is our contention that if our major educational goal, as a society, is to prepare handicapped and disadvantaged youth to assume an adult role in our culture as participating citizens, then there should be fewer philosophical differences between the two fields of career education and vocational education. Since both fields *share the common goal* of helping youth become productive adults, we feel that one approach cannot be successful in meeting this objective without the other.

Vocational Educators	*Career Educators*
I'm primarily concerned with the psychomotor skills for specific jobs.	I address all the career/life skills, cognitive, affective, and psychomotor.
I believe that only qualified vocational instructors should be involved.	I believe that every teacher has a responsibility to provide appropriate career education.
I work only with high school or post-high school age students.	I work with every teacher from kindergarten through college; career education is lifelong.
My job is to help meet the labor market needs of our country.	My job is to help the student become a productive member of society by meeting his/her needs.
I'm only interested in training my students for paid employment.	I'm interested in paid employment but there are also skills to be learned from unpaid employment.
I can describe my program in detail in terms of specific courses and programs.	I can describe career education best as a process, a philosophy, and a method for enhancing each individual's career development lifelong.
I focus on the best ways to learn specific skills that I have learned in the past.	I'm interested in helping students develop general career skills that may be applied in unknown careers in the future.
I'm basically content oriented. Every student *must* know the bottom line.	I'm basically interested in knowing whether the content meets the individual's needs.

Figure 1. Philosophical differences between career education and vocational education.

From our own practical experience, another factor that should be considered in developing a new definition is the importance of helping youth like Scott achieve an acceptable life-style. To do this, the educational and ancillary programs designed to help Scott must focus on the *real* problems that prevent learning handicapped and disadvantaged youth from becoming participating members of our society – the many barriers to employment that may exist *anywhere* in our society.

Thus, our definition of *career/vocational education for mildly learning handicapped and disadvantaged youth:*

> **Any activity, program, course, or service provided by the schools, family, industry, business or the community that is designed to break down the barriers to employment for the handicapped and disadvantaged citizens of our country.**

This definition includes training in specific skills for specific occupations as well as the broad approach of assisting handicapped and disadvantaged persons to acquire general life and work skills for successful adjustment to our everchanging work-oriented society.

BARRIERS TO EMPLOYMENT

What are the barriers to employment of mildly learning handicapped and disadvantaged students? Figure 2 lists the five major barriers including examples and, with the exception of the last barrier, sample solutions.

Economic factors are always hotly debated by the leading contenders in our presidential elections. We as educators can do little in the larger sense about the economy except vote. However, with the exception of the economic factors, the other major barriers to employment can be addressed *directly* by vocational educators, manpower trainers, special educators, counselors, and other program specialists.

There are any number of works that deal with the interventions to assist the vocational student in overcoming the actual physical disability or disadvantage itself. Therefore, this text will not address this barrier to employment directly. Chapter 5, in dealing with the development of an effective "work personality," addresses the barrier

BARRIER	EXAMPLES OF BARRIER	SAMPLE SOLUTION(S)
DISABILITY OR DISADVANTAGE ITSELF	Physically unable to perform the tasks for specific job.	Alternate, appropriate job choice; prosthesis.
	Lack of personal funds for appropriate professional training.	Scholarship; federal loans.
ATTITUDES OF SOCIETY AND EMPLOYERS TOWARDS	"Handicapped workers just can't cut it." "Those kids will steal us blind."	In-service education and "public relations campaigns" aimed at eliminating stereotypical attitudes; laws.
MILDLY LEARNING HANDICAPPED/ DISADVANTAGED YOUTH		
EDUCATION AND TRAINING LIMITATIONS IN THE SYSTEM	Teachers lack skills, technology, and equipment for dealing with these populations.	In-service, skill-oriented education for teachers; research on better methods and equipment.
ATTITUDES OF THE DISABLED OR DISADVANTAGED PERSON	"I just can't do it." "Why should I?"	Career education; counseling, psychological services; better training for teachers.
ECONOMIC FACTORS	Unemployment, recession, etc.	No pat answers here.

Figure 2. Barriers to employment of mildly learning handicapped and disadvantaged youth.

concerned with the disabled or disadvantaged student's attitudes. The balance of the book focuses on what we consider to be the major barriers to employment of the handicapped: "Attitudes of Society, Employers, and Teachers" and "Education and Training Limitations." The sections below provide the reader with a framework for our later discussions.

Barriers to Employment: Attitudes of Society, Employers, and Teachers

Almost every book dealing with handicapped or disadvantaged students devotes a portion of its text to a discussion of the historical and current levels of discrimination against such persons and the resulting stereotypical attitudes and behaviors. Such negative attitudes have existed for centuries, especially against groups with highly visible handicaps or minority groups. Various studies have shown that even persons trained and working in the helping professions tend to hold such attitudes (Greer, 1975).

In a recent study, Gardner & Warren (1977) demonstrated that one of the major barriers to employment of learning handicapped (or disadvantaged) students may very well be the attitudes of teachers that stem from a stereotypical misunderstanding of the relationship between vocational training and academic training. They asked 104 teachers from various disciplines, e.g. special education, career education, and vocational education, to estimate the grade level of reading required to learn certain vocational skills and then to estimate the reading level necessary for *job success* using these same skills. They found no significant difference in the ratings made by teachers regardless of the teachers' area or educational background. The majority of the teachers (90%) estimated that at least first grade level reading was required to learn these vocational skills *when in fact no reading was required for learning or performing any of the job tasks.* Moreover, 72 percent of the sample believed that literacy (at least 5th grade reading) is a minimum requirement for learning these same job tasks. Gardner & Warren conclude:

> The onus is upon those who direct university training programs, in-service training programs, and upon practicing educators to acquire more accurate knowledge about occupations for which . . . [the handicapped] . . . can be trained. Moreover, professionals . . . must share the responsibility for helping their colleagues gain a better understanding of the potential . . . [of handicapped persons] . . . for a wide variety of jobs and skills. (Gardner & Warren, 1977, p. 28)

This study is cited here as an illustration of an underlying attitudinal barrier to employment of mildly learning handicapped and academically disadvantaged youth. If teachers (and society) continue to focus their efforts on only the academics of the educational spectrum to the detriment of career/vocational skills training, students such as Scott will continue to suffer.

Moreover, in most urban areas there are a large number of alienated youth whose progress in school is marginal or nonexistent. These students have so-called normal intelligence but in fact function quite similarly in school to mildly learning handicapped students. According to Arrangio (1980),

> the majority of these problem students are those who come from home environments where early experience has left an indelible stamp on them and has handicapped them in their ability to adapt and function successfully as a student in school, and later as an adult in other social, political and economic roles . . . It is not surprising that individuals who come from these homes experience great difficulty in assimilating the goals, institutions, and the life-style of the predominant culture. No wonder they are called by many names: ". . . the uneducables, the nonlearners, the hard-to-reach, the alienated . . ." (Arrangio, 1980, pp. 2-3)

There is no doubt that the "academic bias" of a great many of our teachers plays an important part in their inability to deal with these so-called "nonlearners." If this is true of special educators, vocational educators, and others of whom we would expect enlightened beliefs and attitudes, how can we expect employers to accept the disadvantaged or handicapped worker?

What about employers? Employers are especially sensitive to appearance. They are reluctant to hire employees who have an obvious handicap or who fail to dress in the acceptable mode for their type of business. Petzy (1978) found that the attitudes of first line supervisors, personnel managers, and top management were important determinants in the success of mentally retarded persons on jobs. In their study of employers, Gardner & Warren (1976) found that employers appear to have no clear picture about the work potential of handicapped workers or the differences in type of handicapping conditions.

In summary, these and other misconceptions, on the part of both educators and employers, coupled with general societal stereotyping, permeate our culture. As a result, the attitudes held by society that are related to insufficient understanding of the work and educational potential of the populations discussed in this text represent a major barrier to employment that must be overcome through career/vocational programming if we are to achieve optimal benefits for society and our students.

Much of this problem is amenable to remediation through inservice training. Training must include an emphasis on establishing a strong working relationship between the education and employment sectors. Both educators and employers need to learn the true potential of handicapped and disadvantaged persons and to adopt a broader perspective on job requirements and redesign.

Barriers to Employment: Education and Training Limitations

Anyone with a basic knowledge of the field can probably compile a long list of educational and training barriers to the full employment of learning handicapped and disadvantaged youth. These barriers will range from a lack of appropriate equipment to poor teacher training. Although many of these limitations apply equally to the nonhandicapped, in the case of disadvantaged or learning handicapped students, educational and training barriers can represent hurdles that are almost impossible for them to overcome.

In an effort to address these barriers, two Boston University projects focused on the development of curriculum materials to help overcome some of the training barriers for these students who are enrolled in regular vocational programs (see Gardner & Beatty, 1979; Gardner, Beatty & Warren, 1979; Gardner & Kurtz, 1979a, 1979b). The materials are designed to support the ongoing instruction of the student in his/her vocational program.

The needs assessment that led to the funding of the projects and four years of developmental work found the following:

1. Resource support teachers are responsible for *both* academic and vocational support instruction, although most of the resource personnel are not trained to work in specific trade areas.
2. The teachers charged with supporting the vocational program of the learning handicapped/disadvantaged students had *little or no training in the development of curriculum materials for the vocational or technical content of the trade areas.* The weakness caused by this lack of training is exacerbated by the lack of curriculum materials available for the teachers to use.
3. Vocational teachers have had *little or no training in working with handicapped or disadvantaged youth.* This can be remediated in preservice programs by making course work and practice in special education mandatory for the aspiring vocational teacher. More important, the emphasis on acquiring *practical skills* and knowl-

edge about training these students to become workers should be increasingly a concern of those at the state and federal levels who are responsible for the in-service training of teachers. A program for in-service training designed to include attention to teacher motivational factors and the identification of "innovative" teachers should prove to be an essential component in quality in-service training (Gardner & Beatty, 1980).

4. There was *no provision* in the current school organization for vocational teachers and support personnel to work together on *interdisciplinary teams*. Not only is this a motivational factor in getting teachers involved in curriculum development (Gardner & Beatty, 1980), but it is also a successful management approach for the development of curriculum materials in technical language support (Gardner & Beatty, 1979).

5. Vocational teachers *lacked the skills* to organize, develop, and design curriculum materials that could serve as additional reinforcement and training to help these students succeed in a regular vocational program. This finding is not surprising and is well supported in the literature (e.g. Brolin, 1976; Gardner & Warren, 1978).

What about employers? Are there educational and training barriers affecting the full employment of the handicapped at the job site? The answer, of course, is that there are many factors on the job that may prevent handicapped and disadvantaged students from being successful. These factors, not unlike the ones encountered in the school system, are also amenable to remediation. One form of remediation would be on-site educational programs for supervisors and human resource personnel in the work potential of handicapped persons. Training could also be offered in appropriate and effective supervisory techniques.

Other approaches would include "human engineering" of the job and the work environment to maximize the potential of the individual handicapped or disadvantaged worker. Employers generally are not aware that jobs can be redesigned or restructured to match the skills and potential of handicapped workers (Petzy, 1978). By applying modern task analysis techniques, employers can create individualized jobs for specific handicapped workers that will maximize their contributions to the company's production without sacrificing quality. Hiring practices and policies can be revamped to assist qualified handicapped workers more affirmatively in obtaining employment. Moreover, these procedures can effectively be coordinated with the local school system to help ease the transition from school to work for handicapped students.

The bulk of this text is devoted to ideas on how to deal with many of the barriers to employment for mildly learning handicapped and disadvantaged persons.

DEFINITIONS

As we mentioned earlier in our discussion of Scott, labels change with the times. Scott can be classified either as mildly learning handicapped or as disadvantaged. What we mean by mildly learning handicapped or disadvantaged relates to the potential of the student to achieve full integration in society.

Mildly Learning Handicapped

Our definition of *mildly learning handicapped* covers many children who are labeled mildly mentally retarded or mentally handicapped. All of us in the business of working with students are aware of the problems associated with the use of test scores in labeling. For instance, we know two young men who score about 70 on a standardized IQ test. One functions like a normal person; the other one definitely is "retarded" in the lay sense. Our definition would include the former student but not the latter. Our definition also includes children who are currently labeled learning disabled and mildly emotionally disturbed. In all instances, what we mean by *mildly learning handicapped* is that the students are having difficulty *learning in school* and the root of the problem cannot be attributed to an economic or cultural background. While this definition may be considered to be very broad, it should be viewed within the context of the materials presented in this text. Our purpose is to provide insights and ideas for teachers who work with the largest group of students who are having problems in school and who have at the same time the greatest potential for success after formal schooling ends. Moreover, it has been our experience, as you will see in later chapters, that these students are more alike than they are different.

Disadvantaged Students

Here again, our definition is a broad one. Our purpose is not so much to label students by specific problems or etiology as to ensure that the largest group of students who need help will get it. This definition is really one of subtraction. If a student is having learning problems in school and these cannot be attributed to the operational factors used in your state to define a learning disabled, emotionally disturbed, or mildly mentally retarded student, but rather can be attributed to an economic or cultural background, then this student is labeled "disadvantaged."

At this point, you are probably saying to yourself, What does all this mean? What it means is that children who have learning problems in school that can be considered "mild," regardless of etiology, are the subjects of this text. We honestly do not care how you label them as long as they receive services. One school system we have worked with makes a practice of labeling children either "special education" or "disadvantaged" (assuming the student can be classified legally either way) depending on the amount of state and federal funds available for support services. Figure 3 illustrates our point. It contains the criteria for "labeling" children as either in need of special services from the handicapped law (P.L. 94-142) or from the disadvantaged section of the vocational education law (P.L. 94-482). If you go back and reread our description of Scott you will readily see how one could make a case for placing Scott in either category.

It is not our purpose here to begin a debate over whether or not a student like Scott should be labeled as "special education" or as "disadvantaged." It is our purpose to make the point strongly that mildly learning handicapped and disadvantaged children have similar problems and that the methodology used to support the career/vocational education of either group should be basically the same. Whether Scott is labeled under either category is irrelevant. He is still a student who is having learning and emotional problems. He requires extra support services, both psychological and educational, if he is to succeed in an appropriate career/vocational program.

HOW TO USE THIS BOOK

This book is not designed as a complete work on the career/

SPECIAL EDUCATION "Learned disabled or emotionally disturbed" P.L. 94-142	VOCATIONAL EDUCATION "Disadvantaged" P.L. 94-482
"(i). . . condition exhibiting one or more of the following characteristics over a long period of time and to a marked degree, which adversely affects educational performance:	"(1) Have academic or economic disadvantage. . . (2) require special services . . . to succeed in vocational education. . .
. . .(B) An inability to build or maintain satisfactory interpersonal relationships with peers and teachers. . .	(1) Lacks reading and writing skills. . .
	(3) Performs below grade level. . .
[or]	
. . . a disorder in one or more of the basic psychological processes involved in understanding or in using language, spoken or written, which may manifest itself in an imperfect ability to listen, think, speak, read, write, spell or do mathematical calculations. . ."	(1) Family income is at or below national poverty level. . . (3) Participant or parent of participant is recipient of public assistance. . .etc."

Figure 3. How Scott might fit under both categories for services (P.L. 94-142 versus P.L. 94-482).

vocational education of mildly learning handicapped and disadvantaged youth. Rather this text is a book of readings about how some of the barriers to employment for these youth can be addressed.

For the reader who is just entering the field, this text can serve as an introduction to the career/vocational education of mildly learning handicapped and disadvantaged youth. Also, for the beginning reader, we suggest additional readings, including the following:

Brolin, D.E. *Vocational Preparation of Retarded Citizens*. Columbus, OH: Merrill, 1976.

Brolin, D.E. & Kokaska, C. *Career Education for Handicapped Children and Youth*. Columbus, OH: Merrill, 1979.

Gardner, D.C. & Warren, S.A. *Careers and Disabilities: A Career Edu-*

cation Approach. Stamford, CT: Greylock Pubs, 1978.

For the more experienced practitioner, this text can serve as a reference book to problem solving. Figure 4 outlines the major sections by the barriers to employment that each addresses.

BARRIER(S)	TOPIC	CHAPTER NUMBER
Education & Training Limitations: Attitudes of Employers and Teachers	Assessment and Evaluation: Work Potential and IVEPs	2 and 3
Education & Training Limitations	Curriculum Modification: Teaching Technical Language	4
Education & Training Limitations: Attitudes of Student	Changing the Work Personality	5
Education & Training Limitations: Attitudes of Teachers	Managing Curriculum Change	6
Education & Training Limitations: Attitudes of Society and Employers	Developing an Effective Work Experience Program	7
Education & Training Limitations	Future Programming	8

Figure 4. Barriers to employment addressed by key chapter.

REFERENCES

Arrangio, J. The effects of individual goal-setting conferences and classroom instruction in human relations on locus of control, school attendance and alienation of disadvantaged high school students. Unpublished doctoral dissertation, Boston University, 1980.

Brolin, D.E. *Vocational Preparation of Retarded Citizens.* Columbus, OH: Merrill, 1976.

Brolin, D.E. & Kokaska, C. *Career Education for Handicapped Children and Youth.* Columbus, OH: Merrill, 1979.

Clark, G.M. *Career Education for the Handicapped Child in Elementary Classroom.* Denver, CO: Love, 1979.

Gardner, D.C. Career, vocational, technical education. In Knowles, Asa (Ed.): *International Encyclopedia of Higher Education.* San Francisco, CA: Jossey-Bass, 1978.

Gardner, D.C. & Beatty, G.J. Practical approaches to curriculum development: A management handbook. Final Report, Project HIRE, Vol. 2, USOE Grant No. G007701947, Boston, MA: Boston University, School of Education, June, 1979. *Resources in Education,* August, 1980, ERIC ED 183739.

Gardner, D.C., Beatty, G.J. & Warren, S.A. Vocational curriculum modification: Teaching technical language to learning handicapped students. Final Report, Vol. 1, Project HIRE, USOE Grant No. G00701947, Boston, MA: Boston University, School of Education, September, 1979. *Resources in Education,* August, 1980, ERIC ED 183738.

Gardner, D.C. & Beatty, G.J. Motivating teachers for vocational curriculum development of the handicapped. *Education, 100(4),* Summer, 1980.

Gardner, D.C. & Kurtz, M.A. Evaluation of a curriculum model for teaching phototypesetting to handicapped students. *Education, 99 (3):*314-320, Spring, 1979.

Gardner, D.C. & Kurtz, M.A. Teaching technical vocabulary to handicapped students. *Education, 16 (3):*252-257, Fall, 1979.

Gardner, D.C. & Warren, S.A. *Careers and Disabilities: A Career Education Approach.* Stamford, CT: Greylock Pubs, 1978.

Gardner, D.C. & Warren, S.A. Career education potential for students at the Massachusetts Hospital School in Canton: An evaluation of current programs and proposal for the development and implementation of a career education program. *Resources in Education,* 1976, ERIC ED 117454.

Gardner, D.C. & Warren, S.A. Teachers' knowledge of the relationship between reading and work. *Illinois Career Education Journal, 32(1):* 27-28, 1977.

Greer, B.G. Attitudes of special education personnel toward different types of deviant persons. *Rehabilitation Literature, 36(6):*182-184, 1975.

Hoyt, K.B. *An Introduction to Career Education: A Policy Paper of the U.S. Office of Education.* Washington, D.C.: U.S. Govt. Print. Office, 1975.

Hoyt, K., Evans, R., Mackin, E., & Mangum, G. *Career Education: What Is It and How to Do It,* 2nd ed. Salt Lake City, UT: Olympus Pub Co, 1974.

Marland, S.P. *Career Education: A Proposal for Reform.* New York: McGraw, 1974.

Petzy, V. Employer considerations of job redesign for educable mentally retarded persons. Unpublished doctoral dissertation, Boston College, 1978.

CHAPTER 2

INDIVIDUAL CAREER/VOCATIONAL ASSESSMENT AND PROGRAM EVALUATION

THE terms career/vocational *assessment* and career/vocational *evaluation* are used frequently as interchangeable terms. In fact, there appears to be no commonly accepted definition of either. Our purpose is to distinguish between these two terms for clarification and for ease of understanding. Just as sociology is often referred to as assuming the individual and studying the group while psychology is often described as assuming the group and studying the individual, we refer to *assessment* as primarily concerned with the individual while *evaluation* focuses on the *group* or program.

WHAT IS CAREER/VOCATIONAL ASSESSMENT?

There are, undoubtedly, a multitude of definitions of *assessment.* In this text, we view career/vocational assessment as a problem-solving process that focuses on individual clients or students. The career/vocational assessment process is simply an application of scientific method, which is really organized common sense, to the solving of career/vocational training and placement problems for individual students. It involves the identification of the problem area(s), the formulation of questions, guesses (hypotheses) about the problems identified, and the establishment of remedial and instructional procedures (goals and objectives) designed to solve these problems. Career/vocational assessment is concerned also with predicting training success and employment success about a specific student. There are a number of theoretical assumptions underlying the career/vocational assessment process. These may vary from theorist to theorist, but we espouse the following:

Assumptions in Career/Vocational Assessment

1. The preparation of students or clients for employment and the concomitant process of career/vocational training and counseling is different from preparing a student or client to adjust in other aspects of his or her life, e.g. marriage-family life, the "school environment," community activities. Preparation for work in our society is de facto preparation for the attainment of economic objectives. This occurs in a culture that is work oriented, achievement oriented, and goal directed. The focus is on the achievement of goals, the meeting of deadlines, the completion of tasks, and the relationship of rewards to inputs and outputs. Thus, the focus of career/vocational assessment is on *productive* employment, on helping clients become *productive,* contributing members of our society.

2. The way a person views the world of work and the way he behaves according to his beliefs, attitudes, and views about work are the primary factors that make the differences between success or failure in a work culture. In other words, personality variables are probably the most important variables to be considered in vocational assessment. Most people get fired from jobs because of personality factors and the resultant behaviors (can't get to work on time; can't get along with the boss or fellow employees; won't accept responsibility; etc.) rather than from inability to perform the tasks of the job. The area of the "work personality" is, then, of primary importance in career/vocational assessment and training.

3. Corollary to the assumption of the importance of personality factors for work-related outcomes is the assumption that career development and the concomitant development of the "work personality" are developmental processes. That is, a person's career development and work personality are developed beginning in early childhood and continue to change and develop throughout adulthood. The assumption is also made that appropriate educational and counseling programs can modify a person's career development and work personality (see Hoyt, 1975).

The Goals and Characteristics of Career/Vocational Assessment

1. Career/vocational assessment is *prognostic* in nature. That is, it is oriented towards the future and, thus, asks questions that are pre-

dictive in focus: (a) Can the client learn how to work? (b) What kind of work can the person learn how to do? and (c) What is the most appropriate training or counseling program that will help the person learn how to work?

2. Being future focused, career/vocational assessment is *ahistorical.* It simply is not concerned with the past unless specific past experiences can be used practically to predict future work training and placement potential.

3. Career/vocational assessment is a *matching* process. It determines the vocational strengths and weaknesses of a specific student or client for work and *matches* these against career training and job possibilities.

4. Career/vocational assessment is a *comprehensive* process that uses *work* as the focal point, the *raison d'etre* for the assessment.

5. Career/vocational assessment is also an *exploration* process. A carefully planned career/vocational assessment for a specific client or student not only collects useful information for career decision making for the individual, it concurrently helps the student/client learn more about himself or herself in terms of interest, abilities, work tolerance, etc., as related to job selection.

6. Career/vocational assessment is *specific* and *individually* oriented. It should always lead to the development of a specific, individualized career/vocational plan.

7. Career/vocational assessment usually involves *teamwork.* A thorough assessment system may involve an *interdisciplinary* team approach that may include teachers, trainers, counselors, social workers, psychologists, medical personnel, etc., as well as the student/client and, if appropriate, the student's parents.

8. Career/vocational assessment should be viewed as an *ongoing process.* The process continues periodically throughout the training period. It ends when the student or client makes a successful adjustment to work.

Types of Assessment Approaches

Generally, career/vocational assessment can take a variety of forms. It can focus on psychological testing, job analysis, work sampling, situational assessment, or criterion-referenced assessment. Usually, a comprehensive career/vocational assessment for a mildly learning handicapped or disadvantaged person will incorporate many of the approaches listed above. These approaches are discussed later on. All of these approaches will ask one or more of the following questions: (1) How does Scott compare to other people working in a specific occupational area? (2) What is the probability that Scott will be successful if he trains for that specific occupational area? (3) Of the occupational areas that we have tried to match with Scott's skills, interests, and abilities, which one is the best match? (4) Of those occupational areas for which he seems best suited, which one will make him feel and act optimally given his own "work personality?"

WHAT IS CAREER/VOCATIONAL EVALUATION?

Like assessment, career/vocational evaluation is a process. Also like assessment, there is a plethora of definitions of evaluation in the literature. Definitions range from conservative (evaluation deals only with answering the specific question of whether or not the program did what it said it was going to do) to more liberal, goal-free approaches (evaluation asks what happened as a result of the program or treatment regardless of intent).

In our text, career/vocational evaluation refers to the process of making judgments about career/vocational programs for mildly learning handicapped and disadvantaged students and clients. The process may have several components.

Components of a Career/Vocational Program Evaluation

1. An ideal career/vocational evaluation will begin before a program is implemented. It will include, in this first phase, a determination of factors that may affect outcomes of the program. It will include a description of the total *environment* in which the program will be offered. This portion of the evaluation includes but is not limited to an accurate description of the *population* that will be serviced, a statement of the *need and problem area(s),* and a description of possible *constraints* on program implementation, e.g. funding, community resources, staffing.

2. In the next phase, the evaluation will focus on the *identification of goals and objectives,* including specification of realistic and practical

approaches to meeting these goals and objectives (operational objectives and strategies). This phase also includes *making decisions* about which alternatives to select for program implementation. In other words, the evaluator, after helping the program personnel refine their objectives and specify the possible ways in which these objectives can be made, will then assist them in deciding which is the best and most practical alternative to select for implementation.

3. The next phase of the evaluation process is sometimes referred to as the *process evaluation*. In this phase, the evaluator asks the question, How is the program being implemented? This is a monitoring phase that concerns itself with the administrative system of the program. How well is the project going operationally? The evaluator may make suggestions for modifications throughout the project's duration. The evaluator is concerned with collecting from various sources data such as information on number of students not being serviced, those being serviced, the expenditures on equipment, per pupil costs, attendance and attrition rates, etc.

4. The fourth component, often referred to as the *product evaluation* phase, is concerned with the *products or outcomes* of the training/treatment. The evaluator asks the *key questions:* (1) Were the objectives met? (2) If so, to what extent were they met? and (3) What was the "cause" of the outcome(s)? This is usually determined inferentially. That is, improvements are usually inferred to be the effects of the program.

5. The last component of an ideal career/vocational program evaluation is the *reporting* stage. The evaluator usually furnishes a written report that describes the events, expenditures, staff, population, etc. Simply stated, the evaluator reports in writing what happened (clients learned 50 new technical terms), to whom it happened (20 learning handicapped students in culinary arts), where and when it happened (last semester in the resource room), and under what conditions (special instructional packages administered individually). The evaluator's report will also contain (usually) probable explanations for what happened (causal-inferential statements) and recommendations for changes or modification in the program based on the findings of the evaluation. The report may also make recommendations for new approaches.

A CAREER/VOCATIONAL INDIVIDUAL ASSESSMENT AND PROGRAM EVALUATION MODEL

Both assessment and evaluation use the same tools, e.g. tests, logic, and design, and both are concerned with improving the career/vocational education for mildly learning handicapped and disadvantaged persons. The difference between the two approaches is largely one of focus. Assessment in career/vocational education focuses primarily on the question, What will happen if we put Scott in culinary arts? while evaluation focuses on the question, What happened to the group of students (including Scott) who received training in the 10th grade culinary arts program last semester? However, evaluation may also concern itself with the question, What did in fact happen to Scott last semester in the culinary arts class? We prefer to use the term *reassessment* rather than evaluation when career/vocational personnel ask this question. Reassessment is used to see if a particular student made gains. Evaluation asks a global question about the average effects of a program on a group of students. Figure 5 illustrates our process.

WHO NEEDS IT

In our work with vocational teachers and others in the field of career/vocational education we often find them "turned off" to the notion of assessment and evaluation. The general feeling among practitioners seems to be "What do I need this stuff for . . . it's just so much jargon. Let's get on with the real business of education. Just give me the equipment, etc. and I'll turn out the best group of workers you ever saw!" No doubt there is some truth in this typical approach. Unquestionably, there never seems to be enough help, time, or money for teachers to accomplish their goals. However, assessment and evaluation have much to offer teachers (and of course students). Assessment can be useful to teachers in helping them solve the basic problem of understanding the individual student. It can provide valuable information on which methods of teaching hinder or help the student to learn the cognitive, motor, and affective skills he/she will need to master to become employable. It can provide information on learning deficits, learning styles and motivation, interest, and attitudes. It can explain to the teacher

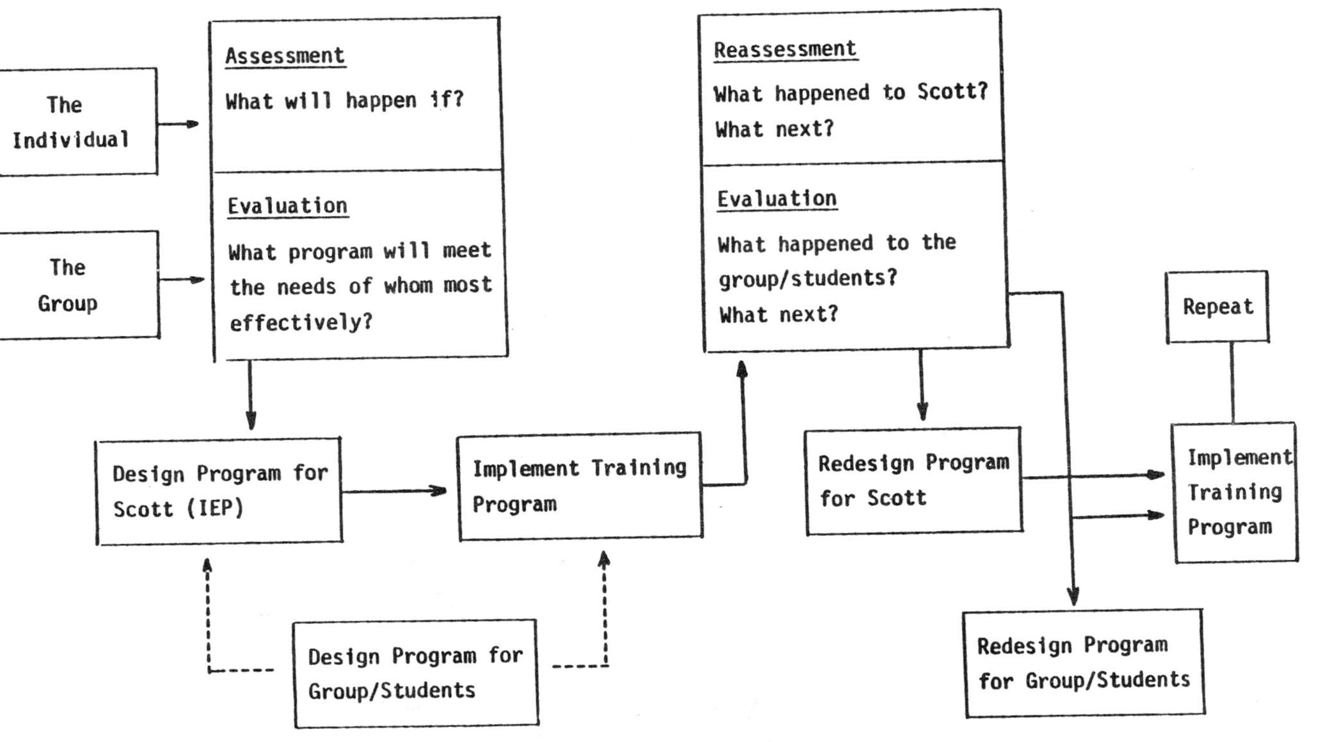

Figure 5. Individual career/vocational assessment and program evaluation process.

why a specific child is not learning what is being taught as well as why the student is not applying the knowledge. It can also provide information on how to organize the classroom flexibly so that there is a balance of individual versus group interactions that will maximize and facilitate the learning process for all the students. It will help the teacher focus on specific areas for the development of new strategies based on "hard" data.

Assessment and evaluation will help the teacher find out not only how effective his teaching approaches are but also which method is better on specific topics. Assessment data can also be useful in helping the teacher to select multimedia equipment and materials. It also gives very specific information about individual and group progress. It may also provide pertinent information about probable causes of student learning problems that are beyond the control of the vocational teacher, e.g. home problems and cultural barriers, and that can be addressed by other specialists in the school. Moreover, the results of a formal assessment lead to the teacher receiving help in the form of technical assistance, new equipment, support services for the student, classroom aides, etc.

Assessment and evaluation, from the point of administration, are important components of the management system. Properly evaluated programs are easier to defend against budget cuts and ensure that the taxpayers (and the students) are getting their money's worth. In the case of programs for handicapped students, properly executed individual assessments ensure that the school is well protected in case of lawsuits from parents or agencies under P.L. 94-142. If the student has been properly assessed and his/her programs evaluated periodically (IEP developing and monitoring), then more than likely the student will be well served and there will be no need for legal intervention. Such a system also serves as a protection for the teacher responsible for the education of the specific learning handicapped student.

THE AREAS AND TOOLS OF INDIVIDUAL CAREER/VOCATIONAL ASSESSMENT AND PROGRAM EVALUATION

The balance of this chapter is devoted to a brief discussion of areas of assessment and evaluation and brief descriptions of sample instruments and approaches for assessment and evaluation activities. This chapter in no way purports to be a complete treatise on the subject but instead should be considered a brief introduction to the subject for teachers and other professional personnel whose role in the career/vocational education of the students is more instructional than clinical. The instruments listed and discussed in the following section were selected from a pool of instruments examined by Project VITA (Gardner & Kurtz, 1977; Warren & Gardner, 1977), a federally funded vocational education project. Additional instruments the authors have used in practice are also included.

Warren & Gardner (1977) reviewed a list of 108 instruments that appeared to have potential usefulness in assessment and evaluation for those personnel involved in career/vocational education of learning handicapped and disadvantaged youth (as defined in our text). The criteria they used to make the final selection of instruments to be used in their report were as follows:

1. Potential for use in individual career/vocational assessment.
2. Potential for use in curriculum development and evaluation.
3. Appropriate grade-age levels (adolescents and adults).
4. Review of instruments suggested potential usefulness for individual assessment or program evaluation. Focus was on prediction of success for vocational training.
5. Acceptable, reported reliability and validity.*
6. Individual features of instruments indicating appropriateness for the population, e.g. designed for nonreaders.

Intelligence Testing

Intelligence tests are concerned with measuring intellectual and cognitive abilities. They are concerned with measuring the various components of intelligence, such as verbal ability, numerical ability, nonverbal, conceptual, or reasoning ability, spatial relations, vi-

***Reliability:* The term reliability is used to describe the accuracy of a test. It refers to the consistency and stability of the test. Reliability addresses the question of whether one can "trust" or "believe" in an individual student's score. There are various sophisticated techniques for determining the forms of reliability. The most common is the test-retest approach (stability).

Validity: Validity is concerned with whether the test does what it says it is designed to do. For example, if the aim of the test is to predict academic achievement, then various techniques are used to establish that it does or does not in fact predict academic achievement.

sualization, mechanical comprehension, perceptual speed and accuracy, and memory. The most widely used tests are paper-pencil tests that require reading ability; they may not be useful for learning handicapped populations. The actual total IQ score is not really useful in vocational prediction. However, some of the subtest scores, such as verbal ability, numerical ability, memory, and others are useful. The literature is fairly extensive on this topic, and interested readers will find it helpful to study the research before using intelligence tests for predictions about vocational success and training. Remember that the basic rationale for intelligence tests is to predict *academic* achievement. Some examples follow.

TEST: *Wechsler Intelligence Scales for Children and Adults*

AUTHOR: David Wechsler
PUBLISHER: Psychological Corporation
LEVEL: Children 5 to 15 years, 11 months (WISC); Adult (WAIS)
DESCRIPTION: Has both verbal and performance subtests. Verbal subtests: (1) Information, (2) Comprehension, (3) Arithmetic, (4) Similarities, (5) Vocabulary, and (6) Digit Span. Performance subtests: (1) Picture Completion, (2) Picture Arrangement, (3) Block Design, (4) Object Assembly, and (5) Coding. Minimal to mild corrected vision required; adequate hearing for six verbal subtests; oral speech and no less than moderate hand-arm coordination.
RELIABILITY: Range for all tests, 0.57 to 0.96.

TEST: *Peabody Picture Vocabulary Test*

AUTHOR Lloyd M. Dunn
PUBLISHER: American Guidance Service Inc.
LEVEL: Ages 2.5 to 18
DESCRIPTION: This is a measure of verbal intelligence only. Caution should be used in equating this with the processes measured by the longer and more variegated scales.
RELIABILITY: .67 at 6 years of age to .84 at 18 years

Achievement Testing

Achievement testing is becoming an increasingly controversial area in education. Many schools have eliminated achievement testing, while others still maintain that it has some validity for measuring school outcomes. Achievement tests are designed to measure the scope and depth of student academic achievement in such areas as reading level, spelling level, arithmetic level, and ability to follow written and/or oral instructions. Most standardized achievement tests have national norms and good to excellent reliability/validity. For the populations emphasized in this text, mildly learning handicapped and disadvantaged youth and adults, the results of academic achievement testing may yield very little useful information from the perspective of predicting vocational employment or vocational training success. However, they can be used to determine deficiency areas that relate to a specific job's academic requirements, e.g. reading level for technical information. An example of an achievement test follows. There are, of course, others that the school psychologist might want to select for specific reasons.

TEST: *Test of Adult Basic Education* (TABE) (1976 Edition)

AUTHOR:	Modification of 1970 California Achievement Test
PUBLISHER:	CTB/McGraw-Hill
LEVEL:	High School through Adult, Reading levels grades 2-4, 4-6, 6-9
DESCRIPTION:	Achievement tests in reading, mathematics, and language.

Aptitude Testing

Aptitude testing is a logical approach to predicting work success. However, there is some controversy on the usefulness of aptitude tests. It is not our purpose to enter the debate on testing in this text but to point out that those who plan to use aptitude tests should be cautious about the validity of their inferences and should make a point of carefully studying the literature in this area. Aptitude tests range from tests for a specific occupation, such as salesperson, to tests of manual skill and dexterity, to general aptitude batteries that test verbal ability, math ability, clerical speed and accuracy, reasoning, and other general skills. Some of the paper-pencil tests are not appropriate for some learning handicapped students. The tests on manual skill and dexterity apparently are more useful with retarded and physically handicapped populations than with persons of normal intelligence. Most persons with normal intelligence who do not have physical disabilities usually have average or better manual skills. Examples of aptitude tests follow.

A. Specific Occupations

TEST: *Computer Programmer Aptitude Battery*

AUTHOR: J.M. Palormo
PUBLISHER: Science Research Associates, Inc.
LEVEL: Young adults (applicants for training or employment as a computer programmer)
DESCRIPTION: Six scores: (1) Verbal Meaning, (2) Reasoning, (3) Letter Series, (4) Number Ability, (5) Diagramming, and (6) Total Score. For use with applicants for computer training or employment. Correlations of total test score with grades in computer training range from .46 to .71. Tasks and tests have close correspondence to the tasks of programming.
RELIABILITY: .67 to .94 (Split half, KR- 20) .95 (estimated total)

TEST: *Detroit Retail Selling Inventory*

AUTHORS: H.J. Baker & P.H. Bolker
PUBLISHER: Public School Publishing Company
LEVEL: Secondary students and young adults
DESCRIPTION: Five scores: (1) Personality, (2) Intelligence, (3) Checking, (4) Arithmetic, and (5) Total Score. For use with students in secondary schools who are considering retail sales training and for inexperienced applicants for retail selling jobs in business.
RELIABILITY: .76 to .98

B. Aptitude Batteries

TEST: *Differential Aptitude Test,* 2nd Edition, 1962

AUTHOR: G.K. Bennett, H.G. Seashore & A.G. Wesman

PUBLISHER: Psychological Corporation

LEVEL: Grades 8 through 12 and Adults

DESCRIPTION: Consists of eight tests: (1) Verbal Reasoning, (2) Numerical Ability, (3) Abstract Reasoning, (4) Clerical Speed and Accuracy, (5) Mechanical Reasoning, (6) Space Relations, (7) Language Uses: Spelling and (8) Language Uses: Grammar. Norms available on approximately 50,000 boys and girls representing a cross section of the U.S.

RELIABILITY: .87 to .94 (except for Mechanical Reasoning, which, for girls, is reported as low as .70.)

TEST: *General Aptitude Test Battery*

AUTHOR: None

PUBLISHER: U.S. Employment Service, Government Printing Office

LEVEL: Grade 12 and Adults

DESCRIPTION: Nine factors: (1) Intelligence, (2) Verbal Aptitude, (3) Numerical Aptitude, (4) Spatial Aptitude, (5) Form Perception, (6) Clerical Perception, (7) Motor Coordination, (8) Finger Dexterity, (9) Manual Dexterity. Raw scores can be converted to percentile ranks or standard scores; standard scores can be compared with over thirty-six occupations' aptitude patterns in over 800 jobs.

RELIABLITY: .80 to .90 (test-retest, parallel forms)

TEST: *Non-Reading Aptitude Test Battery*

AUTHOR: None

PUBLISHER: U.S. Employment Service, Government Printing Office

LEVEL: Grades 9 through 12, Adults (disadvantaged)

DESCRIPTION: This test is a nonreading adaptation of the General Aptitude Test Battery. It has fourteen tests, nine scores: (1) Numerical, (2) Intelligence, (3) Verbal, (4) Spatial, (5) Clerical, (6) Perception, (7) Form Perception, (8) Finger Dexterity, (9) Motor Coordination, (10) Paper-pencil test and four Performance tests.

RELIABILITY: For research purposes only

*C. Mechanical Ability**

TEST: *Bennett Mechanical Comprehension Test*

AUTHOR: G.K. Bennett & W.A. Ownes

PUBLISHER: Psychological Corporation

LEVEL: Grades 9 through 12, Adults

DESCRIPTION: A revision of the Test of Mechanical Comprehension, Forms AA, BB, W1. Designed to measure the ability to understand and perceive the relationship of physical forces and mechanical elements in practical situations.

RELIABILITY: .81 to .93 (internal consistency)

TEST: *Chriswell Structure Dexterity Test*

AUTHOR: M.I. Chriswell

PUBLISHER: C.H. Stoelting Company, Vocational Guidance Service

LEVEL: Grades 8 and 9

DESCRIPTION: Designed to measure structure dexterity, which is defined as ability to translate the visualization of structures into specific motor responses. This is analogous, or closely related, to interpreting blueprints through appropriate manual bench and machine work.

RELIABILTY: .86 (test-retest)

*See also subtests of Differential Aptitude Test

D. Manual Dexterity

TEST: *Crawford Small Parts Dexterity Tests*

AUTHOR: J.E. Crawford & J.M. Crawford
PUBLISHER: Psychological Corporation
LEVEL: High School and Adults
DESCRIPTION: Two scores: (1) Pins and Collars, and (2) Screws. Designed to measure fine eye-hand coordination as related to assembly and adjustment of such devices as electronic equipment, electric clocks, hearing aids, and the manipulation of small hand tools. Low correlation between parts 1 and 2 (.10 to .50). Norms are provided for several groups: students, job applicants, and employees.
RELIABILITY: Part 1: .80 to .91 Part 2: .90 to .95

TEST: *Hand Tool Dexterity Test*

AUTHOR: G.K. Bennett
PUBLISHER: Psychological Corporation
LEVEL: Adolescents and Adults
DESCRIPTION: A work sample test designed to measure proficiency in the use of ordinary tools such as a screwdriver or wrench. Norms available on a large sample of males from a paper factory.
RELIABILITY: .91 (test-retest)

TEST: *Purdue Pegboard*

AUTHOR: J. Tiffin (Purdue Research Foundation)
PUBLISHER: Science Research Associates
LEVEL: Ages 9 through 16, Adults
DESCRIPTION: Five scores: (1) Left Hand, (2) Right Hand, (3) Both Hands, (4) Right plus Left, plus Both Hands, (5) Assembly. Designed to aid in selecting employees for industrial jobs requiring manipulative dexterity. Purports to measure gross movements of both fingers and hands and arms and tip of the finger dexterity.

RELIABILITY: .60 to .76

Personality, Interest, and Other Testing

Even a novice in career/vocational education is aware that "personality" factors are the most critical element in whether or not a person is successful occupationally. Most people who are fired are fired for personality factors, however defined. Unfortunately, most assessment programs shy away from personality assessment. There are many reasons for this. First, most personality measures require reading, and for many learning handicapped and disadvantaged students this presents a problem. Another factor is that such testing by and large remains in the domain of clinical psychologists and psychiatrists and, frankly, is expensive. Moreover, many educators feel uncomfortable dealing with these problems. In point of fact, however, educators deal with these problems on a daily basis, e.g. in the form of behaviors and attitudes. There is one area that offers promise for direct application to career/vocational training — the application of locus of control change techniques and career maturity change techniques to educational and on-the-job training settings. Three measures are presented below as examples, two that measure locus of control and one that measures career maturity. More detailed information on the reliability and validity of these instruments is contained in Appendix A.

Logically, one should also be concerned in assessment and evaluation with measuring students' occupational interests, since this is a basic component of career/vocational motivation. Many interest measures rely heavily on reading and are not useful for some learning handicapped and disadvantaged youth. A number of picture inventories have been designed to address this problem. They are rather new and should be used with caution. Examples of interest inventories and other measures are shown.

TEST: *Career Maturity Inventory*

AUTHOR: J.O. Crites
PUBLISHER: CTB/McGraw-Hill
LEVEL: Grades 6 through 12 (Note: Adult form available)
DESCRIPTION: Consists of (I) Attitude Scale and (II) five competence tests in a research edition. The

five competence tests are (1) Self-Appraisal, (2) Occupational Information, (3) Goal Selection, (4) Planning, (5) Problem Solving (see Chapter 4 and Appendix A).

RELIABILITY: (I) Attitude Scale: .74 (KR-20)
(II) Competence Test: .72 to .90 (with exceptions). Two low coefficients were reported for Problem Solving subtest in the sixth and the seventh grades.

TEST: *Different Situations Inventory, Self Report Form*

AUTHOR: David C. Gardner & Sue Allen Warren

PUBLISHER: David C. Gardner & Sue Allen Warren

DESCRIPTION: Twenty-item paper and pencil measure, forced choice format. Designed to measure a person's generalized expectancy for reinforcement (locus of control) (see Chapter 4 and Appendix A).

RELIABILITY: .90 (test-retest)

TEST: *Different Situations Inventory, Rater Form*

AUTHOR: David C. Gardner & Sue Allen Warren

PUBLISHER: David C. Gardner & Sue Allen Warren

DESCRIPTION: Twenty-item paper and pencil measure, forced choice rating form. Items identical to Self Report Form. Designed to obtain a rating of an individual's generalized expectancy for reinforcement (locus of control) as estimated by a supervisor, counselor, or teacher (see Chapter 4 and Appendix A).

RELIABILITY: .86 (internal consistency)

TEST: *Work Situations Inventory*

AUTHOR: David C. Gardner, Grace Joely Beatty & Margaret A. Kurtz

PUBLISHER: David C. Gardner, Grace Joely Beatty & Margaret A. Kurtz

DESCRIPTION: Ten-item paper and pencil, forced choice, self-report form. Designed to measure specific locus of control of reinforcement in work-related and career-related activities. Still in the experimental stage (see Chapter 4 and Appendix A).

RELIABILITY: .70 (internal consistency)

TEST: *Picture Interest Inventory*

AUTHOR: K.B. Weingartan

PUBLISHER: CTB/McGraw-Hill

DESCRIPTION: Nine scores: (1) Interpersonal Service, (2) Mechanical, (3) Natural, (4) Business, (5) Esthetic, (6) Scientific, (7) Verbal, (8) Computational, (9) Time Perspective. Nonverbal inventory. Closely related to the Occupational Interest Inventory.

RELIABILITY: .69 to .92 (test-retest)

TEST: *Reading Free Interest Inventory*

AUTHOR: R.L. Becker

PUBLISHER: American Association on Mental Deficiency

LEVEL: Adolescents and adults educably mentally retarded

DESCRIPTION: Designed as a nonreading measure of vocational preference for educably mentally retarded youth in specific job areas. Job areas selected on basis of realistic potential for EMR. Eleven categories for males and eight for females.

RELIABILITY: Males: .68 to .92 (KR-20); .75 to .92 (test-retest) Females: .69 to .96 (KR-20); .72 to .88 (test-retest)

TEST: *Geist Picture Interest Inventory*

AUTHOR: Harold Geist

PUBLISHER: Western Psychological Services

LEVEL: Ages 8 through 16, Adults

DESCRIPTION: Eighteen scales for males and nineteen scales for females; twelve interest scores: (1) Clerical, (2) Mechanical, (3) Musical, (4) Scientific, (5) Outdoor, (6) Persuasive, (7) Literary, (8) Computational, (9) Artistic, (10) Social Service, (11) Dramatic, (12) Personal Services (females only). Seven motivation scores: (1) Family, (2) Prestige, (3) Intrinsic and Personality, (4) Environmental, (5) Financial, (6) Past Experience, (7) Could not say. Test is a pictorial approach for young people and others who have difficulty with verbal materials.

RELIABILITY: .57 to .73 (median r, test-retest, $N = 1659$)

TEST: *Geist Picture Inventory: Deaf Form: Male*

AUTHOR: Harold Geist
PUBLISHER: Western Psychological Services
LEVEL: Ages 7 through 16 and Adults
DESCRIPTION: For deaf and hard of hearing males. Adaptation of the Geist Picture Inventory. Ten scores: (1) Clerical, (2) Mechanical, (3) Persuasive, (4) Outdoor, (5) Scientific, (6) Literary, (7) Artistic, (8) Computational, (9) Social Service, (10) Dramatic.
RELIABILITY: .53 to .57

TEST: *Kuder General Interest Survey*

AUTHOR: G.F. Kuder
PUBLISHER: Science Research Associates, Inc.
LEVEL: Grades 6 through 12
DESCRIPTION: This is an extension of the Kuder Preference Record Vocational Form C. Eleven Scores: (1) Mechanical, (2) Outdoor, (3) Scientific, (4) Computational, (5) Artistic, (6) Persuasive, (7) Literary, (8) Musical, (9) Clerical, (10) Social Service, and (11) Verification. This version of the Kuder Preference Record Vocational Form C was developed for use with junior high school level children and is written at a *sixth grade reading level*.
RELIABILITY: Above .70 (KR-20)

TEST: *Kuder Preference Record Vocational (Form C)*

AUTHOR: G.F. Kuder
PUBLISHER: Science Research Associates, Inc.
LEVEL: Grades 9 through 12 and Adults

DESCRIPTION: Ten interest scales: (1) Mechanical, (2) Outdoor, (3) Scientific, (4) Computational, (5) Artistic, (6) Persuasive, (7) Literary, (8) Musical, (9) Clerical, (10) Social Service. Also provides a score on Verification. Offers percentile ranks for males and females. Stanines for women and men in forty-one occupational clusters.

RELIABILITY: .47 to .75 (test-retest)
KR for 10 scales in 70s and 80s

TEST: *Ohio Vocational Interest Survey*

AUTHOR: A.G. D'Costa, D.W. Winefordner, J.R. Odgers & P.B. Koones, Jr.

PUBLISHER: Harcourt Brace Jovanovich, Inc.

LEVEL: Grades 8 through 12

DESCRIPTION: Cannot be scored locally. Twenty-four scores: (1) Machine Work, (2) Manual Work, (3) Personal Services, (4) Caring for People or Animals, (5) Inspecting and Testing, (6) Clerical Work, (7) Crafts and Precise Operations, (8) Customer Services, (9) Skilled Personnel Services, (10) Nursing and Related Technical Services, (11) Training, (12) Numerical, (13) Literary, (14) Appraisal, (15) Applied Technology, (16) Agriculture, (17) Promotion and Communication, (18) Supervision and Management, (19) Artistic, (20) Music, (21) Entertainment and Performing Arts, (22) Sales Representative, (23) Teaching - Counseling - Social Work, (24) Medical. National standardized sample of 45,000 students, grades 8 through 12.

RELIABILITY: .80 (test-retest)

TEST: *Pictorial Interest Inventory*

AUTHOR: B.B. Scarborough

PUBLISHER: B.B. Scarborough

LEVEL: Adult males, *nonreaders* or *poor readers*

DESCRIPTION: *For research purposes only.* Eleven scores: (1) Personal Service, (2) Protective and Custodial, (3) Clerical and Sales, (4) Mechanical, (5) Farming, (6) Building and Maintenance, (7) Vehicle Operators, (8) Skilled-Sedentary, (9) Electrical Workers, (10) Assembly Line Workers, and (11) Natural Processors.

RELIABILITY: For research purposes only

TEST: *Strong Vocational Interest Blank for Men*

AUTHOR: Edward K. Strong, Jr., D.P. Campbell, R.F. Birdie & K.E. Clarke

PUBLISHER: Stanford University Press

LEVEL: Ages 16 and over

DESCRIPTION: Eighty-four scales: (1) twenty-two basic interest scales, (2) fifty-four occupational scales, (3) eight nonoccupational. Also, six administrative indices.

RELIABILITY .90 (test-retest) (30 days)

TEST: *Strong Vocational Interest Blank for Women*

AUTHOR: E.K. Strong, Jr. & D.P. Campbell

PUBLISHER: Stanford University Press

LEVEL: Ages 16 and over

DESCRIPTION: Eighty-one scales: (1) nineteen on basic interest, (2) fifty-eight on occupational and (3) four nonoccupational. Also, six administrative indices.

RELIABILITY: .68 (test-retest)

JOB ANALYSIS AND WORK SAMPLE APPROACH TO ASSESSMENT

Anyone who has had an introductory course in industrial psychology has a fairly good notion of the job analysis approach used by industry and business for many years. Job analysis is simply a process of studying, observing, and interviewing workers to determine and delineate the important activities of workers on specific jobs. Job analysis describes the important requirements and the technical and environmental aspects of the job and identifies and describes the specific tasks, skills, knowledge, abilities, and responsibilities required for the employee to obtain successful job performance levels.

Within the context of individual career/vocational assessment and evaluation, job analysis is not, per se, an assessment and evaluation methodology. However, an assessment specialist, armed with the specificity of job requirements developed in a job analysis, can use this information to develop a matching process of specific job tasks to specific abilities of individuals who have the appropriate skills and/or who have the potential to be trained to acquire such skills. It is at this point that the assessment specialist may integrate information from psychological and educational testing in a comprehensive individual assessment. Job analysis data may also be used in developing work samples.

There is much controversy about the work sample approach to career/vocational assessment, and there is no doubt that this approach is not as efficient as an actual job tryout in the real world for an individual client or student. This approach is, however, a more practical answer for many vocational assessment personnel to their increasing dissatisfaction with the psychological testing models. Work sampling assessment lies somewhere on the spectrum between actual job tryouts and psychological assessment. At its best, work sampling combines the best features of both methodologies. Work samples or job samples are simulated or miniature work situations. In many instances, they are made up of actual job tasks that the client would have to perform on a specific job.

The advantages of an approach that combines job analysis and a work sample are obvious and practical. Much of the appeal lies in that the assessment and evaluation process deals with *concrete* tasks, situations, and operations that are either analogous to or, in fact, actual reproductions of the tasks that the student or client must perform on the job. Thus, inferences are directly related to the real world of work. For the student or client being examined, the motivation is built-in. Mildly learning handicapped and disadvantaged youth are simply more "turned on" to real life, meaningful, and relevant tasks. Moreover, direct observation of the client performing the job sample tasks gives more information and more relevant work-task performance data than other methods. Since the job/work sample approach eliminates any criticism of cultural or other biases and since it uses an approach similar to job analysis, it is more appealing to employers.

There are a number of recognized problems with the job/work sample approach, however. Most critics complain, justifiably, that few agencies or firms using job/work samples bother to establish reliability or validity on their work samples. Since the purpose of the work sample assessment is the same as psychological assessment, *prediction,* such a criticism is reasonable and valid. Other problems with the job/work sampling approach are cost, increased time involved, early obsolescence, the need for trained personnel, the issues of which of the many tasks involved in a given job to choose, and that it ignores the "personality and attitudinal factors" of prediction of job success.

The number of job/work samples is myriad, the majority of which are developed locally by agencies providing services. There are also numerous commercial versions, many of which are *very expensive.* The samples on the following pages are presented as an *illustration* from a typical commercial catalogue. The reprinting of them here in no way implies the endorsement of the authors. Those planning to use the job/work sample approach are cautioned to seek reliability and validity data from the publisher(s) and/or to hire professional specialists to devise and validate in-house work samples.

1. METAL CONSTRUCTION WORK SAMPLE

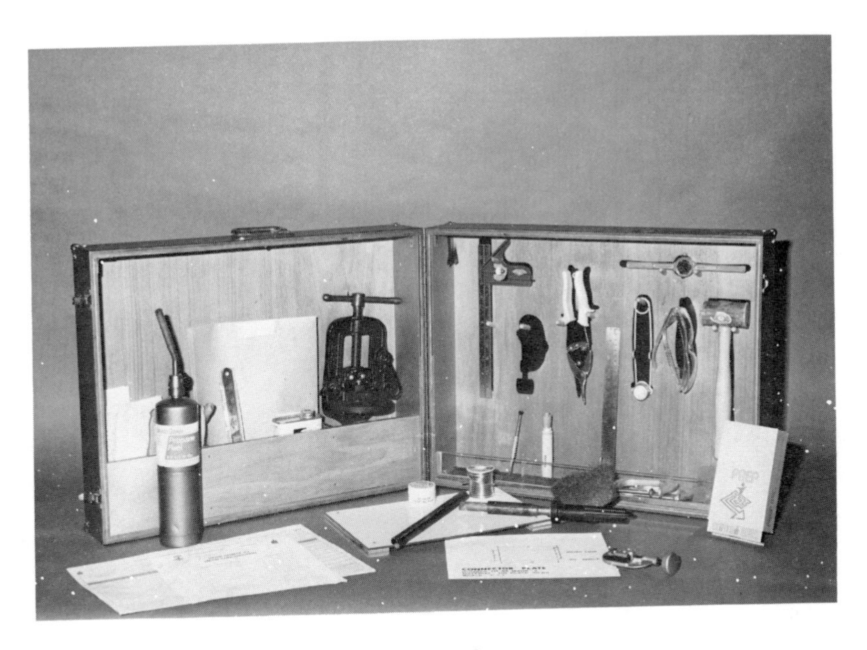

Figure 6.

Synopsis

Assessment and Exploration Work Sample

The Metal Construction Work Sample is designed to help individuals explore their interest and aptitude levels for jobs in a fast growing industry of the 1980s. They will be introduced to –

- JOB OPPORTUNITIES OF THE FUTURE
- EDUCATIONAL AND TRAINING REQUIREMENTS
- WORKING CONDITIONS AND ENVIRONMENT
- METAL CONSTRUCTION TERMINOLOGY
- METAL CONSTRUCTION EQUIPMENT

This information is incorporated into a series of hands-on activities, providing the individual with a sampling of the work he or she would encounter in this vocation. These are –

- MEASURING AND LAYOUT
- CUTTING STOCK PHYSICALLY
- BENDING AND SHAPING STOCK
- ASSEMBLING COMPONENTS PHYSICALLY
- ASSEMBLING BY SOLDERING

The activities are explained in detailed, step-by-step instructions displayed on an easy-to-use audiovisual projector. There are no time restrictions on the individual to complete the tasks. The average completion time is two hours and six minutes.

During the program, the individual evaluates his or her interest and ability related to each activity. This information is combined with the instructor's comments on the performances to create an evaluation of the individual's job potential in the metal construction field. A specific Instructor's Guide explains setup of the program, evaluation points and criteria, and statistical support information for the program. Training is available on the evaluation and interpretation of these results and is recommended for the instructor.

MODE OF PRESENTATION — Audiovisual, 16 mm filmstrip and audiotape package in self-contained cartridge

---

Reprinted with the permission of Prep, Inc., 1575 Parkway Avenue, Trenton, New Jersey.

WORK SAMPLE EQUIPMENT & MATERIALS	Soldering Iron Propane Torch Vise Combination Square Aviation Snips Scribe C Clamps Tube Cutter Die & Die Stock Mallet File Angle Iron	Work Gloves Copper Tubing Flux & Brush Cutting Oil Steel Wool Sheet Metal Plates Steel Rods Solder Safety Glasses One (1) audiovisual cartridge Instructor's Guide Program Forms
PACKAGING	Self-contained storage cube with latch holds all equipment and forms Weight when full: 59 lbs. Storage container dimensions: 26"L x 8½"W x 20"H Reorders for the consumable materials are available in units of ten	
OTHER EQUIPMENT NEEDED (purchased separately)	PREP Projector with 7" x 5" screen Table: 48"W x 30"D x 30"H	
TIME REQUIRED TO ADMINISTER	Average completion time two hours and six minutes for one cartridge Work Sample can be scheduled by individual tasks	
EVALUATION MATERIAL (purchased separetely)	Individual Self-Rating Forms for student response Evaluator's Report Form (hand scored) for evaluator's objective comments and scoring related to student's work performances and work behavior Packaged together in units of ten	
TRAINING FOR INSTRUCTORS/ EVALUATORS	Recommended Available at PREP, Inc. during scheduled inservice sessions, or at your site	

The contents of this program have been researched and developed based on Dictionary of Occupational Titles:

D.O.T. CODE	*TITLE*
804.281	Sheet Metal Worker
619.686	Sheet Metal Shop Helper
810.384	Arc Welder
810.684	Gas Welder
819.384	Combination Welder
813.684	Brazer
862.381	Plumber
862.884	Pipe Fitter Assistant

Growth in these occupations for the 1980s is expected to increase by 35 percent to 49 percent.

2. SMALL ENGINE WORK SAMPLE

Figure 7

Synopsis

Assessment & Exploration Work Sample

The Small Engine Work Sample is designed to help individuals explore their interest and aptitude levels for jobs in a growing industry of the 1980s. They will be introduced to —

- JOB OPPORTUNITIES OF THE FUTURE

- EDUCATIONAL AND TRAINING REQUIREMENTS
- WORKING CONDITIONS AND ENVIRONMENT
- SMALL ENGINE TERMINOLOGY
- SMALL ENGINE EQUIPMENT

This information is incorporated into a series of hands-on activities, providing the individual with a sampling of the work he or she would encounter in this vocation. These are –

- PERFORMING OIL CHANGE
- PERFORMING AIR CLEANER MAINTENANCE
- TESTING ELECTRICAL SYSTEM
- PERFORMING SPARK PLUG MAINTENANCE
- PERFORMING COMPRESSION TEST AND RECORDING COMPRESSION READING

The activities are explained in detailed, step-by-step instructions displayed on an easy-to-use audiovisual projector. Since there are no time requirements on these tasks, the equipment allows the individual to set the pace of the program, though the average completion time is one hour and twenty-three minutes.

During the program, the individual evaluates his or her interest and ability related to each activity. This information is combined with the instructor's comments on the performances to create an evaluation of the individual's job potential in the small engine field. A specific Instructor's Guide explains setup of the program; evaluation points and criteria; and statistical support information for the program. Training is available on the evaluation and interpretation of these results and is recommended for the instructor.

MODE OF PRESENTATION	Audiovisual, 16 mm filmstrip and audiotape package in self-contained cartridge	
WORK SAMPLE EQUIPMENT & MATERIALS	4-Cycle Engine	Oil
	Spark Plug Gapping Tool	Cleaning Solvent
	Compression Gauge	Washing Pan
	Screwdriver	Funnel
	7/16" Wrench	Program Forms
	3/4" Deep Well Socket	One (1) audiovisual cartridge
	3/8" Drive Ratchet	Instructor's Guide
	Wire Brush	

PACKAGING	Self-contained storage cube with latch holds all equipment and forms Weight when full: 80 lbs. Storage container dimensions: 26"L x 15³/₈"W x 20"H Reorders for the consumable materials are available in units of ten
OTHER EQUIPMENT NEEDED (purchased separately)	PREP Projector with 7" x 5" screen Table: 48"W x 30"H x 29"H
TIME REQUIRED TO ADMINISTER	Average completion time is one hour and twenty-three minutes for one cartridge Work Sample can be scheduled by individual tasks
EVALUATION MATERIAL (purchased separately)	Individual Self-Rating Forms for student response Evaluator's Report Form (hand scored) for evaluator's objective comments and scoring related to student's work performances and work behavior Packaged together in units of ten
TRAINING FOR INSTRUCTORS/ EVALUATORS	Recommended Available at PREP, Inc. during scheduled inservice sessions, or at your site

The contents of this program have been researched and developed based on Dictionary of Occupational Titles:

D.O.T. CODE	*TITLE*
620.281	Motorcycle Repairperson
625.281	Powersaw Mechanic
623.261	Outboard Motor Mechanic
623.261	Outboard Motor Tester
625.281	Lawnmower Repairperson

Growth in these occupations for the 1980s is expected to increase by 15 percent to 25 percent.

3. BARBERING/COSMETOLOGY WORK SAMPLE

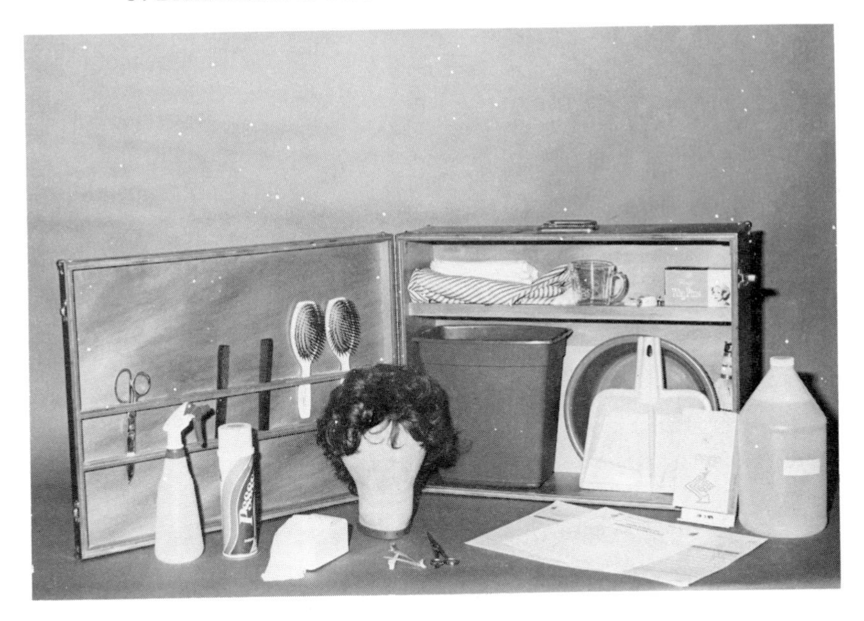

Figure 8

Synopsis

Assessment and Exploration Work Sample

The Barbering/Cosmetology Work Sample is designed to help individuals explore their interest and aptitude in a growing industry of the 1980s. He or she will be introduced to –

- JOB OPPORTUNITIES OF THE FUTURE
- EDUCATIONAL AND TRAINING REQUIREMENTS
- WORKING CONDITIONS AND ENVIRONMENT

- BARBERING/COSMETOLOGY TERMINOLOGY
- BARBERING/COSMETOLOGY EQUIPMENT

This information is incorporated into a series of hands-on activities, providing the individual with a sampling of the work he or she would encounter in this vocation. These are –

- ADMINISTERING BASIC HAIRCUT
- PERFORMING A DRY SHAMPOO
- MEASURING HEAD FOR FITTING WIG
- CLEANING A WIG
- PERFORMING A SALES FUNCTION
- WRITING UP SALES SLIP

The activities are explained in detailed, step-by-step instructions displayed on an easy-to-use audiovisual projector. Since there are no time requirements on these tasks, the equipment allows the individual to set the pace of the program, though the average completion time is one hour and thirty-one minutes.

During the program, the individual evaluates his or her interest and ability related to each activity. This information is combined with the instructor's comments on the performances to create an evaluation of the individual's job potential in the barbering/cosmetology field. A specific Instructor's Guide explains setup of the program; evaluation points and criteria; and statistical support information for the program. Training is available on the evaluation and interpretation of these results and is recommended for the instructor.

MODE OF PRESENTATION	Audiovisual, 16 mm filmstrip and audiotape package in self-contained cartridge	
WORK SAMPLE EQUIPMENT & MATERIALS	Scissors	Wig Cleaner
	Combs	Rubber Gloves
	Brushes	Barber Towels
	Tape Measure	Barber Cape
	Measuring Cup	Program Forms
	Wig	One (1) audiovis-

Dry Shampoo
Whisk Broom & Dust Pan

ual cartridge
Instructor's Guide

PACKAGING

Self-contained storage cube with latch holds all equipment and forms

Weight when full: 53 lbs.

Storage container dimensions: 26"L x 8 1/2"W x 20"H

Reorders for the consumable materials are available in units of ten

OTHER EQUIPMENT NEEDED
(purchased separately)

PREP Projector with 7" x 5" screen
Table: 48"W x 30"D x 29"H

TIME REQUIRED TO ADMINISTER

Average completion time is one hour and thirty-one minutes for one cartridge

Work Sample can be scheduled by individual tasks

EVALUATION MATERIAL
(purchased separately)

Individual Self-Rating Forms for student response

Evaluator's Report Form (hand scored) for evaluator's objective comments and scoring related to student's work performances and work behavior

Packaged together in units of ten

TRAINING FOR INSTRUCTORS/ EVALUATORS

Recommended
Available at PREP, Inc. during scheduled inservice sessions, or at your site

The contents of this program have been researched and developed based on Dictionary of Occupational Titles:

D.O.T. CODE	*TITLE*
330.371	Barber
331.674	Manicurist
332.271	Cosmetologist
332.271	Hair Stylist
332.361	Wig Dresser
339.371	Scalp Treatment Operator

Growth in these occupations for the 1980s is expected to increase by 15 percent to 25 percent.

4. WOOD CONSTRUCTION WORK SAMPLE

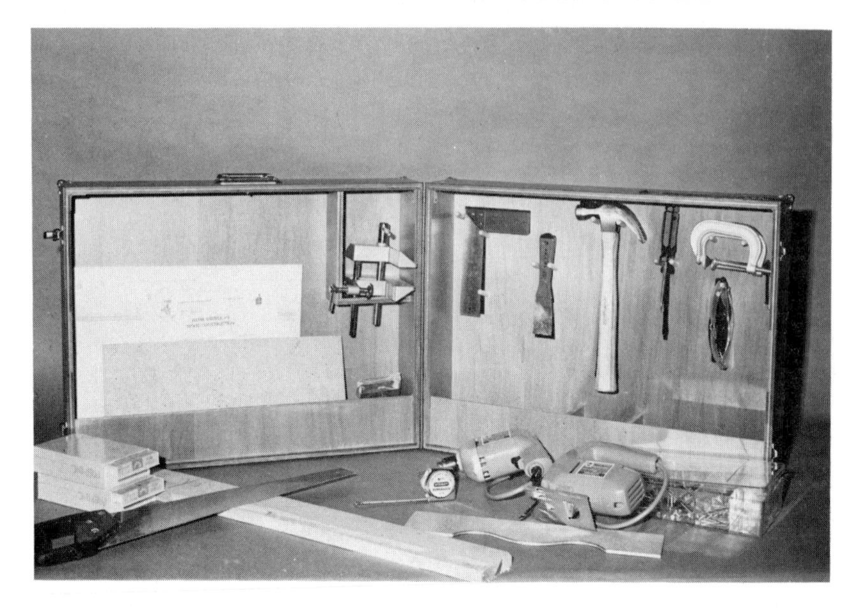

Figure 9

Synopsis

Assessment and Exploration Work Sample

The Wood Construction Work Sample is designed to help individuals explore their interest and aptitude levels for jobs in a growing industry of the 1980s. They will be introduced to —

- JOB OPPORTUNITIES OF THE FUTURE
- EDUCATIONAL AND TRAINING REQUIREMENTS
- WORKING CONDITIONS AND ENVIRONMENT
- WOOD CONSTRUCTION TERMINOLOGY
- WOOD CONSTRUCTION EQUIPMENT

This information is incorporated into a series of hands-on activities, providing the individual with a sampling of the work he or she would encounter in this vocation. These are —

- PERFORMING PRECONSTRUCTION LAYOUT
- MEASURING AND LAYOUT
- CONSTRUCTING WOOD FRAMES

- CONSTRUCTING INTERIOR TRIM
- MAINTAINING AND OPERATING POWER TOOLS & EQUIPMENT

The activities are explained in detailed, step-by-step instructions displayed on an easy-to-use audiovisual projector. Since there are no time requirements on these tasks, the equipment allows the individual to set the pace of the program, though the average completion time is two hours and thirteen minutes.

During the program, the individual evaluates his or her interest and ability related to each activity. This information is combined with the instructor's comments on the performances to create an evaluation of the individual's job potential in the wood construction field. A specific Instructor's Guide explains setup of the program; evaluation points and criteria; and statistical support information for the program. Training is available on the evaluation and interpretation of these results and is recommended for the instructor.

MODE OF PRESENTATION	Audiovisual, 16 mm filmstrip and audiotape package in self-contained cartridge	
WORK SAMPLE EQUIPMENT & MATERIALS	Crosscut Saw Hammer Try Square Bench Vise Tape Measure Screwdriver Putty Knife Saber Saw Electric Drill C Clamps	Wood 8d Nails Sandpaper Plastic Wood Safety Glasses Flat Head Screws Pressboard Program Forms Two (2) audiovisual cartridges Instructor's Guide
PACKAGING	Self-contained storage cube with latch holds all equipment and forms Weight when full: 124 lbs. (Wood packaged separately) Storage container dimensions: 26"L x 8½"W x 20"H Reorders for the consumable materials are available in units of ten	
OTHER EQUIPMENT	PREP Projector with 7" x 5" screen	

NEEDED (purchased separately)	Table: 48"W x 30"D x 29"H
TIME REQUIRED TO ADMINISTER	Average completion time two hours and thirteen minutes for cartridges A & B. Individually: Cartridge A = 71 minutes, Cartridge B = 62 minutes Work Sample can be scheduled by individual tasks
EVALUATION MATERIAL (purchased separately)	Individual Self-Rating Forms for student response Evaluator's Report Form (hand scored) for evaluator's objective comments and scoring related to student's work performances and work behavior Packaged together in units of ten
TRAINING FOR INSTRUCTORS/ EVALUATORS	Recommended Available at PREP, Inc. during scheduled inservice sessions, or at your site

The contents of this program have been researched and developed based on Dictionary of Occupational Titles:

D.O.T. CODE	*TITLE*
860.381	Carpenter – Construction
860.381	Carpenter – House
860.381	Carpenter – Finish
860.781	Carpenter – Form Setter
869.664	Carpenter – Helper and Laborer

Growth in these occupations for the 1980s is expected to increase by 15 percent to 25 percent.

5. FOOD PREPARATION WORK SAMPLE

Figure 10

Synopsis

Assessment and Exploration Work Sample

The Food Preparation Work Sample is designed to help individuals explore their interest and aptitude levels for jobs in one of the fastest growing industries of the 1980s. They will be introduced to –

- JOB OPPORTUNITIES OF THE FUTURE
- EDUCATIONAL AND TRAINING REQUIREMENTS
- WORKING CONDITIONS AND ENVIRONMENT
- FOOD PREPARATION TERMINOLOGY
- FOOD PREPARATION EQUIPMENT

This information is incorporated into a series of hands-on activities, providing the individual with a sampling of the work he or she would encounter in this vocation. These are –

- PREPARING CAKE FROM RECIPE
- PREPARING PERCOLATOR FOR COFFEE MAKING
- CALCULATING PORTIONS AND RECIPE INCREASES

- CALCULATING NUMBER OF SERVINGS PER CAKE OF SPECIFIC SIZE
- PREPARING CAKE FROSTING
- PREPARING HOT SANDWICH

The activities are explained in detailed, step-by-step instructions displayed on an easy-to-use audiovisual projector. Since there are no time requirements on these tasks, the equipment allows the individual to set the pace of the program, though the average completion time is three hours and fourteen minutes.

During the program, the individual evaluates his or her interest and ability related to each activity. This information is combined with the instructor's comments on the performances to create an evaluation of the individual's job potential in the food preparation field. A specific Instructor's Guide explains setup of the program; evaluation points and criteria; and statistical support information for the program. Training is available on the evaluation and interpretation of these results and is recommended for the instructor.

MODE OF PRESENTATION	Audiovisual, 16 mm filmstrip and audiovisual package in self-contained cartridge	
WORK SAMPLE EQUIPMENT & MATERIALS	Measuring Utensils Spatula Timer Mixing Whip Toaster Oven Electric Griddle Coffee Pot Mixing Bowls Dish Pans Cooling Rack Omelette Ingredients	Plastic Wrap Cake Pans Flour, Sugar Coffee Cups Toothpicks Knife, Fork Recipes Dishwashing Liquid Frosting Ingredients Program Forms Instructor's Guide Two (2) audiovisual cartridges
PACKAGING	Self-contained storage cube with latch holds	

	all equipment and forms Weight when full: 93 lbs. Storage container dimensions: 26"L x 15 7/8"W x 20"H Reorders for the consumable materials are available in units of ten
OTHER EQUIPMENT NEEDED (purchased separately)	PREP Projector with 7" x 5" screen Table: 48"W x 30"D x 29"H
TIME REQUIRED TO ADMINISTER	Average completion time three hours and fourteen minutes for cartridges A & B. Individually: Cartridge A = 89 minutes, Cartridge B = 105 minutes Work Sample can be scheduled by individual tasks
EVALUATION MATERIAL (purchased separately)	Individual Self-Rating Forms for student response Evaluator's Report Form (hand scored) for evaluator's objective comments and scoring related to student's work performances and work behavior Packaged together in units of ten
TRAINING FOR INSTRUCTORS/ EVALUATORS	Recommended Available at PREP, Inc. during scheduled inservice sessions, or at your site

The contents of this program have been researched and developed based on Dictionary of Occupational Titles:

D.O.T. CODE	*TITLE*
313.381	Pastry Cook
315.381	Cook
317.684	Sandwich Person
317.687	Cook's Helper
317.384	Salad Person
318.687	Kitchen Helper
319.474	Fountain Person
526.381	Baker

Growth in these occupations for the 1980s is expected to increase by 25 percent to 40 percent.

6. MEDICAL SERVICES WORK SAMPLE

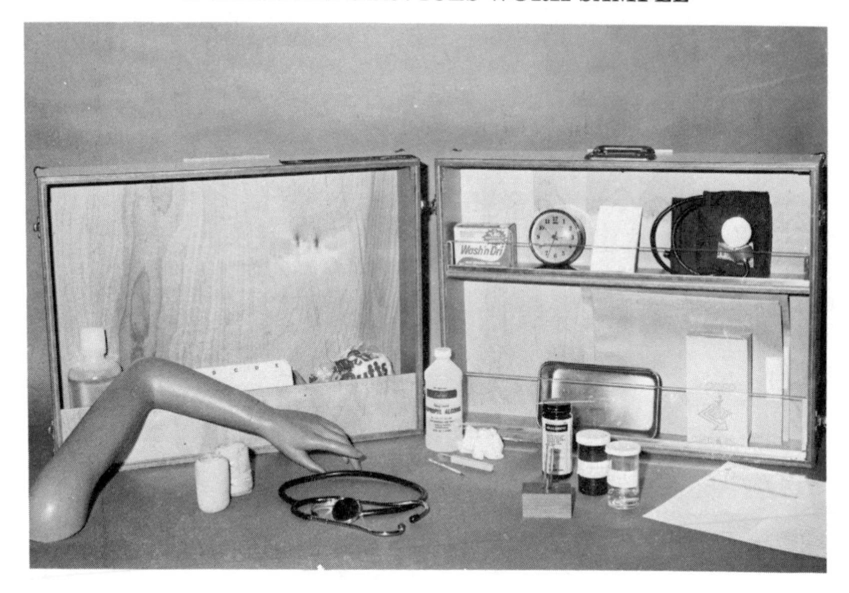

Figure 11

Synopsis

Assessment and Exploration Work Sample

The Medical Services Work Sample is designed to help individuals explore their interest and aptitude levels for jobs in a fast growing industry of the 1980s. They will be introduced to –

- JOB OPPORTUNITIES OF THE FUTURE
- EDUCATIONAL AND TRAINING REQUIREMENTS
- WORKING CONDITIONS AND ENVIRONMENT
- MEDICAL SERVICES TERMINOLOGY
- MEDICAL SERVICES EQUIPMENT

This information is incorporated into a series of hands-on activities, providing the individual with a sampling of the work he or she would encounter in this vocation. These are –

- TAKING AND RECORDING A PATIENT'S VITAL SIGNS
- BANDAGING LIMBS WITH ELASTIC BANDAGES
- PERFORMING CLERICAL TASKS

- OBSERVING AND RECORDING PATIENT'S LIQUID INTAKE & OUTPUT
- PERFORMING AND RECORDING URINALYSIS

The activities are explained in detailed, step-by-step instructions displayed on an easy-to-use audiovisual projector. Since there are no time requirements on these tasks, the equipment allows the individual to set the pace of the program, though the average completion time is one hour and six minutes.

During the program, the individual evaluates his or her interest and ability related to each activity. This information is combined with the instructor's comments on the performances to create an evaluation of the individual's job potential in the medical services field. A specific Instructor's Guide explains setup of the program; evaluation points and criteria; and statistical support information for the program. Training is available on the evaluation and interpretation of these results and is recommended for the instructor.

MODE OF PRESENTATION	Audiovisual, 16 mm filmstrip and audiovisual package in self-contained cartridge	
WORK SAMPLE EQUIPMENT & MATERIALS	Thermometer Test Tubes Stethoscope Sphygmomanometer Ace® Bandages Cotton Alcohol	Billilastix® Sterile Towels Forms Alphabet Dividers Program Forms Instructor's Guide One (1) audiovisual cartridge
PACKAGING	Self-contained storage cube with latch holds all equipment and forms Weight when full: 40 lbs. Storage container dimensions: 26"L x 8½"W x 20"H Reorders for the consumable materials are available in units of ten	
OTHER EQUIPMENT NEEDED (purchased separately)	PREP Projector with 7" x 5" screen Table: 48"W x 30"D x 29"H	
TIME REQUIRED TO ADMINISTER	Average completion time one hour and six minutes for one cartridge	

	Work Sample can be scheduled by individual tasks
EVALUATION MATERIAL (purchased separately)	Individual Self-Rating Forms for student response
	Evaluator's Report form (hand scored) for evaluator's objective comments and scoring related to student's work performances and work behavior
	Packaged together in units of ten
TRAINING FOR INSTRUCTORS/ EVALUATORS	Recommended Available at PREP, Inc. during scheduled inservice sessions, or at your site

The contents of this program have been researched and developed based on Dictionary of Occupational Titles:

D.O.T. CODE	*TITLE*
078.361	Dental Hygienist
078.381	Clinical Lab Assistant
079.371	Dental Assistant
079.367	Medical Assistant
079.374	Licensed Practical Nurse
355.674	Nursing Aide
355.674	Ward Orderly

Growth in these occupations for the 1980s is expected to increase by 25 percent to 40 percent.

SITUATIONAL ASSESSMENT

Situational assessment approaches are concerned with observing the student's or client's behaviors in a work setting to assess the "work personality" as it relates to work attitudes, work behaviors, and work motivation (career maturity). Situational assessment lends itself to numerous approaches including cooperative education, career exploration, work study, and observations made in "sheltered" settings. The approach asks the question whether the student/client/ worker can in fact function effectively on the job. As proponents of "experiential" education, we find this approach exceptionally appealing. However, human behaviors are exceedingly complex, and when studied in real life situations the problem of quantifying subjective data is even more complex. Most assessment specialists use rating scales and similar devices to record and quantify the multivariate behaviors of workers on the job. Recognizing that situational assessment approaches will always be somewhat confounded by the well-known limitations of rating scales, one can use this approach with students or clients for whom other methods of assessment are less effective. In dealing with the work personality, we recommend, at least for mildly learning handicapped and disadvantaged youth, a preventive and instructional approach rather than an assessment one. In Chapter 4, we *assume* deficits in work personality (locus of control and career maturity) and recommend the adaption of instructional and counseling treatments for all clients to reinforce appropriate work attitudes and behaviors and to develop these in students who lack them.

REFERENCES

Gardner, D.C. & Kurtz, M.A. Vocational curriculum models and assessment procedures handbook for handicapped students. Final Report: Project VITA. Boston, MA: Boston University, 1977, USOE Grant No. G00750058.

Hoyt, K.B. *An Introduction to Career Education. A Policy Paper of the U.S. Office of Education.* Washington, D.C.: U.S. Govt. Print. Office, 1975.

Warren S.A. & Gardner, D.C. Vocational training for disabled students: A handbook on assessment. Boston, MA: Boston University, 1977. *Resources in Education,* 1980, ERIC ED 176 040.

CHAPTER 3

CURRICULUM MODIFICATION: TEACHING RELATED SKILLS

"I don't know."
"What does that word mean?"
"I know how to do it but I can't remember all those words."
"I asked my reading teacher to help me with the words but she doesn't know anything about welding."

THESE little scenarios are common in many vocational schools today. Many students can master the skill but can't seem to learn the *related academics* of the trade. Moreover, many resource room specialists are not trained and equipped to deal with related instruction.

One solution to the problem, of course, is to offer teacher training programs for resource specialists so that they may gain both an understanding of dealing with specific learning problems and also a working knowledge of vocational education. In recent years there has been a trend for many schools of education to offer such programs. For instance, Boston University was one of the first to do so beginning in 1974. In the intervening years, a number of private and state colleges have followed suit.

Another solution is the development of instructional materials for use by specialists to assist learning handicapped and disadvantaged youth. This chapter describes materials that were developed in federal projects (e.g. Gardner, Beatty & Warren, 1981; Gardner & Kurtz, 1979a, 1979b). It should be pointed out, however, that the materials described in this chapter are not comprehensive and it may be many years before comprehensive sets of self-instructional packages are available for the numerous trade areas/training programs into which mildly learning handicapped and disadvantaged persons are currently being mainstreamed. The focus, then, for the interested reader should be on studying the *process* used to develop these materials. School systems can do much to encourage interdisciplinary teams of resource room specialists and vocational teachers to work together using this process to make effective in-house materials for specific trade areas.

Before we begin to discuss the process used to develop materials appropriate for mildly learning handicapped and disadvantaged students, let us take a brief look at the special support needed by these students within a vocational high school.

Vocational Mainstreaming in Perspective

Wolfensberger (1972) defines the "normalization principle" as a method or means "to establish and/or maintain personal behaviors and characteristics that are as culturally normative as possible" (p.28). What he means is that when you apply the "normalization principle" to the total life-style of a mildly learning handicapped or disadvantaged person, you should use as a rule of thumb the idea that facilities, educational programming, social activities, etc., for these students should *emphasize providing a normal environment for them.* While there is some controversy over what the words *normal* and *normalization* mean (see Warren, 1973), the principle of normalization is "gaining momentum throughout the country" (Brolin, 1976, p. 37). Moreover, mainstreaming in the public schools is congruent with the normalization principle (Brolin, 1976).

In other words, when you apply the normalization principle in the public school you are "mainstreaming." Simply stated, mainstreaming is a deliberate and conscious application of the normalization principle in public schools. It gives emphasis to placement of learning handicapped and disadvantaged students into the *least restrictive* educational program that is appropriate to their individual needs.

From an administrative viewpoint, mainstreaming can be viewed as a management system. The management system's problems consist of answering the following two questions about each student:

1. What is the least restrictive educational program appropriate for this student?
2. What support services need to be given to this student to ensure that he/she can be successful in the least restrictive environment?

Mainstreaming, contrary to the beliefs of many, does not "mean that every student must be placed in regular classes full time" (Dahl, Appleby & Lipe, 1978). What it means is that the school must provide supportive services, supplemental instructional programs and other part-time services to help individual students "learn alongside their normal peers." Moreover, for mainstreaming programs to be effective, they must be sensitive to the needs of individual teachers. Placing a student in a program without adequate support services, without providing the teacher with additional training, and without an adequate budget for curriculum and equipment modifications is a ludicrous situation. Yet this remains a fear, and a justified one, for most vocational teachers. The problems associated with mainstreaming in vocational education go beyond those of the typical high school. In a regular high school, the bulk of the expenditures for supportive services center on *academic* instructional support.

In most vocational schools, the problems of mainstreaming are multiplied by the uniqueness of vocational education's delivery system and its instructional objectives. In addition to being concerned with the delivery of traditional high school *academics,* the vocational school must also provide support services for the *shop or laboratory* portion of the program as well as for the *trade-related* instruction:

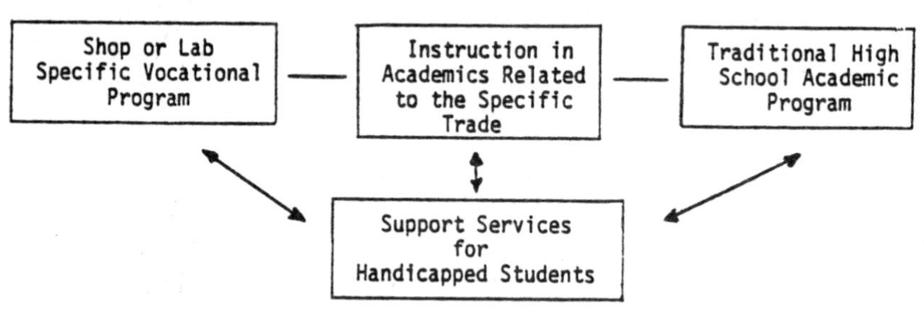

Figure 12. Demands made on support services in a typical vocational program.

For a mainstreaming system to be effective in vocational education, the management system must provide support for the traditional *academic* instruction as well as the *vocational* training program and related instruction. An effective vocational mainstreaming program for mildly learning handicapped and disadvantaged students should include the following:

1. Vocational teachers must be provided with appropriate inservice training, which will help them acquire more positive

and appropriate attitudes towards mildly learning handicapped and disadvantaged students.

2. Vocational teachers must be provided with additional information about the vocational potential and capabilities of individuals who have learning problems.
3. Vocational schools must provide services and personnel who can assess the vocational potential of students like Scott (Chapter 1). The results of the assessment must be translated into meaningful educational and vocational objectives and programming.
4. Vocational schools must develop their own IVEP program and referral system to maximize the vocational education of the individual students.
5. Vocational schools must provide special equipment and modifications in the vocational curriculum to accommodate these students.
6. Vocational teachers, ancillary personnel, and resource room specialists must be given the time and the opportunity to work together to accomplish the goal of helping learning handicapped and disadvantaged students be successful in vocational education.

Curriculum Modification: A Learning Model for Teaching Technical Language

A recent professional estimate indicates that one in five of our seventeen-year-olds in America is a functional illiterate. A recent study in Florida found that

> many students are having difficulty with basic learning skills such as reading and math . . . [and that there is] a wide range of reading abilities among vocational students with a substantial percentage being reading-limited learners . . . who are not functional illiterates . . . but who are unable to comprehend a considerable part of their reading materials . . . [Thus] in order to ensure a high probability of student success . . . it is essential that vocational teachers increase their awareness of, and competency to deal with, students' reading and math . . . deficiencies. (Redmann, 1979, pp. 14-15)

Undoubtedly, there are a myriad number of ways that one could approach this problem. The approach that we are suggesting here is based on our own experience in several projects. The process of curriculum modification and the development of supplementary materials presented here has been field-tested successfully (Gardner, Beatty & Warren, 1981; Gardner & Kurtz, 1979b). In fact this approach has shown such promise (Avallon, 1980; Gardner, Beatty & Warren, 1981) that commercial versions are currently under development.

Learning Model

Most vocational teachers and employers will agree that the ability to understand the essential, entry-level terminology of a specific trade area is a crucial factor in the job success, or failure, of mildly learning handicapped or disadvantaged persons. The ability to master the entry-level mathematics of the trade area is also critical. The curriculum materials described below, the underlying learning principles used to develop the materials, and the basic curriculum development process were field-tested with technical language. It is our contention that the same basic approach and learning principles can also be applied to the development of entry-level mathematics with self-instructional packages for specific trade areas. We suggest, therefore, that the reader study carefully the description of the development of these materials as a *method* that can be applied not only to other language or trade areas but also to the development of materials for helping students master entry-level related mathematics.

Some Assumptions

An assumption of most skill training centers and vocational programs is that students will learn much of the language of the trade "incidentally," that is, that the student will just naturally pick up the trade jargon by being present in the vocational program. However, much research on locus of control has shown that students who tend to be external on locus of control do not learn well incidentally when compared to internals (see Chapter 4). Learning handicapped and disadvantaged students tend to fall in the category of persons with an external locus of control of personality. Thus, most of them do not learn well incidentally and consequently do not "pick it up" in the shop. Consequently, we designed the materials on the assumption that most of the students using them would be reading below grade level and that most of them would not have learned sufficient technical language incidentally.

A third assumption underlying this model was based on recent brain research on hemispheric specialization. According to Wheatley (1977), the

> left hemisphere in normal persons excels in performing routine sequential tasks, logical reasoning, and analysis of stimulus components. Language is processed in the left hemisphere . . . The right hemisphere processes stimuli all at once rather than sequentially. A complex shape is sensed holistically by the right hemisphere, while the left hemisphere analyzes parts one at a time. The right hemisphere "thinks" in images and the left hemisphere "thinks" in words. Thus, the right hemisphere excels in tasks that are nonverbal in nature. (P. 37)

Wheatley makes the point that, at least in public schools, our society rewards left hemisphere activities and that students who find school irrelevant may very well be *right brain oriented.* Further, he points out that

> there is also evidence that the urban poor tend to be right hemisphere oriented while middle class persons are more left-hemisphere oriented. If this is true, then it would explain why many urban poor do not succeed in our schools and why they claim irrelevancy of many of the tasks asked of them in school. (1977, p. 38)

Accepting the basic assumption that mildly learning handicapped and disadvantaged students as a group have right hemispheric orientation, the materials were designed to incorporate a visual image approach to overcome the left hemispheric bias associated with learning technical vocabulary. Figure 13 illustrates this specialization.

Learning Principles

In addition to the assumption of right hemispheric orientation, the materials also incorporate a number of learning principles that have been established empirically. The model, therefore, is an eclectic one in that we used several theoretical bases as well as empirically based learning principles in the design of the materials. Following is a list of the learning principles used:

1. If materials are meaningful and relevant to the students, learn-

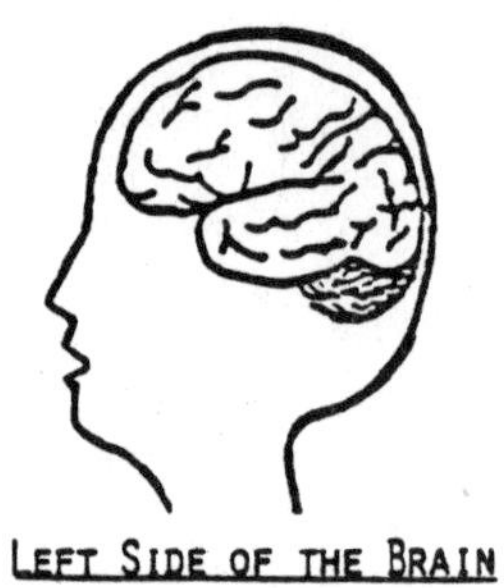

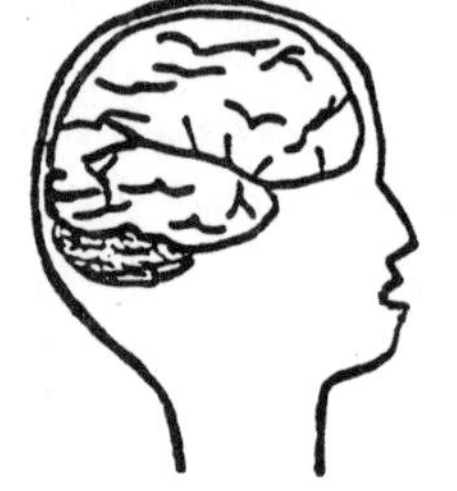

CHARACTERISTICS

Left Side of the Brain	Right Side of the Brain
Thinks in "words" Analyzes the problem Complex shape: analyzes part by part	Thinks in "images" Grasps and solves problems as a whole Complex shape: seen holistically and all at once

FUNCTIONS

Left Side of the Brain	Right Side of the Brain
Language Logical reasoning Routine sequential tasks Analysis of stimuli components	Motor/sensory "Creative side of the brain" Processes sensory information Visualization of three dimensions

GROUP DIFFERENCES

Left Side of the Brain	Right Side of the Brain
Middle class emphasis: over-development of this side in school curricula	Lower SES and handicapped: some children find school "irrelevant" because they prefer right hemisphere learning and tasks.

BI-MODAL MATERIALS

Left Side of the Brain	Right Side of the Brain
Flash cards (written language) Teaching booklet (written language) Tapes (oral language)	Flash cards (illustration/image) Teaching booklet (image) Activities (image focus)

Learning Principles

Interaction

Mastery of Technical Language

Figure 13. Hemispheric specialization.

ing is faster.

2. Learning is best maintained if the material to be learned is used soon after the first learning experience.
3. For mastery of facts, retention is improved and learning is faster if practice learning is distributed during the learning cycle rather than crammed.
4. Clustering the facts to be learned helps the student's retention.
5. Ordering facts and materials to be learned in an easy-to-hard sequence improves learning speed.
6. Retention is improved by overlearning and reviewing facts and materials.
7. Immediate feedback on the correctness of a learning response helps mastery of new terms or facts.
8. Students will learn better if they know part of the task prior to attempting to learn the entire task. (Gardner, Beatty, & Warren, 1979)

The Development Process for Self-Instructional Packages

This section describes the process that we used to develop the instructional packages. The process included the use of interdisciplinary teams of vocational teachers, university personnel, and ancillary personnel from the schools. In most cases, individual teams consisted of a resource room specialist, a vocational instructor, a school administrator, and a university-based coordinator. For a complete description of the management approach, see Chapter 5.

Selection of Content

Since there are hundreds, if not thousands, of technical words or terms in each trade area, we decided that the best approach was to deal with entry-level terminology, since the students using these materials would, almost without exception, begin their careers in entry-level jobs. Also, it is apparent that all students will need to know entry-level terminology before progressing to more advanced concepts.

Once this decision was made, appropriate job descriptions from the *Dictionary of Occupational Titles* were selected. The positions were validated by vocational instructors and employers as being entry-level positions. Then lists were developed of words that were necessary for successful job entry for each of the positions.

Organization of Learning Packages

In the five trade areas in which individualized learning packages were developed (Culinary Arts, Graphic Arts, Arc Welding, Upholstery, and Allied Health), each team chose between 120 and 160 words for inclusion in the packages. It was then necessary to organize the words for each trade area into a manageable, logical format. Our original thought was to organize the words around jobs. This proved to be cumbersome because in many jobs the same tools are used in a number of different tasks. Organizing the words by jobs would have meant that the same tool would have to be defined every single time it was mentioned. Since learning handicapped and disadvantaged students have limited time for resource room instruction, it was decided that a more efficient format was needed. (Note: These materials were designed and field-tested as *supplementary* materials to be used in resource rooms. However, they are equally appropriate for use in the related classroom or as reference material in the vocational shop.)

A further analysis of the terms selected led to the conlusion that there were essentially three types of words or phrases: (1) tools, (2) concepts, and (3) process words. A second attempt at organization of the instructional packages was made on the basis of the types of words. This format was finally rejected when it became apparent that in many cases a specific tool was part of a process or was related to a specific concept. Consequently, the final organization of the learning packages for each trade area was individualized. For example, Culinary Arts was divided into the following sections:

CULINARY ARTS

Teaching Booklet #	*Lesson #*
I. Activities	1. Cutting
	2. Measuring
	3. Mixing
	4. Straining
II. Cooking	5. Turning Foods
	6. Top of Stove Cooking

	7. Storage
	8. Frying and Sautéing
	9. Baking
III. Foods	10. Soups
	11. Vegetables
	12. Sauces
	13. Meat and Fish
	14. Desserts

In Culinary Arts, the words were organized into activities in the first booklet, elementary cooking processes in the second booklet, and basic foods in the third booklet, since most entry-level jobs in Culinary Arts involve either kitchen help or waiter/waitress positions.

In contrast to Culinary Arts, the entire first booklet in Arc Welding was devoted to the concept of safety. When one considers the use of acetylene torches, molten metal, and other dangerous equipment in the Arc Welding program, the format is especially appropriate. The learning packages in Arc Welding were subdivided as follows:

ARC WELDING

Teaching Booklet #	*Lesson #*
I. Safety	1. Inner Garments
	2. Outer Garments
	3. Operation of Equipment
	4. Work Environment
	5. Hazards
II. Equipment/Tools/ Materials	6. Equipment
	7. Electrode Code
	8. Welding Tools
	9. Welding Materials
III. Standard Arc Weld Types	10. Groove Welds
	11. Areas of Measurement
	12. Measurement Tools
	13. Welding Symbols

In summary, each of the five trade areas in which we developed instructional learning packages contained three teaching booklets. The breakdown or format for each trade area, however, was different and specific to the needs of the students in the individual trade area. Three booklets were used, since one teaching booklet of 120 to 160 words would be rather intimidating for any learning handicapped or disadvantaged student. The order of the words within any single teaching booklet was determined by application of the various learning principles mentioned earlier.

Criteria for Development of Definitions and Drawings With Examples

Once the teaching order of the words had been determined, definitions of the terms were written at fourth grade reading levels. Fourth grade level was chosen based on a review of the records of the students in our field test sample. We used the Dale-Chall reading formula and the Dale list of 3,000 familiar words. By constantly consulting the Dale list and substituting acceptable words for more abstract terms, a fourth grade reading level was achieved for all definitions in all trade areas. This particular step proved to be more difficult than we had originally anticipated. For instance, words such as *DC reverse polarity* in Arc Welding involve highly technical concepts that cannot easily be translated into fourth grade vocabulary. For this particular concept, no attempt was made to explain theories of electricity or to give any background to the term. A very elementary definition and an explanation of the effects were included in the final definition:

> **DC reverse polarity** is the kind of electric current that is most often used in arc welding. When you use DC reverse polarity, the electrode is hotter than the work piece.

This definition also illustrates the importance of teaching order in the organization of the instructional packages. The terms *current* and *electrode* had to be defined before *DC reverse polarity,* since both words are used in the definition.

It is also a good example of a continuing problem in the development of the materials: appropriate line drawings. The term *DC reverse polarity* denotes a very technical concept, and finding a single line drawing that adequately illustrated this concept required numerous trials. The real challenge lay in designing a drawing that was representative of the term yet was uncluttered enough for learning handicapped and disadvantaged students. The final drawing and definition (Fig. 14) represent the best compromise. The picture represents the dial on the Arc Welding machine that would have to be turned to DC reverse polarity. The welding teacher would have to demonstrate *how* to turn the dial. Please note that these materials do not attempt to teach *how* to perform tasks; they are designed to reinforce only the vocabulary involved in the process.

Our second basic criteria, then, was to develop one simple and uncluttered line drawing for each definition. The use of the line drawings was obviously based on the hypothesis that right brain stimuli would enhance learning.

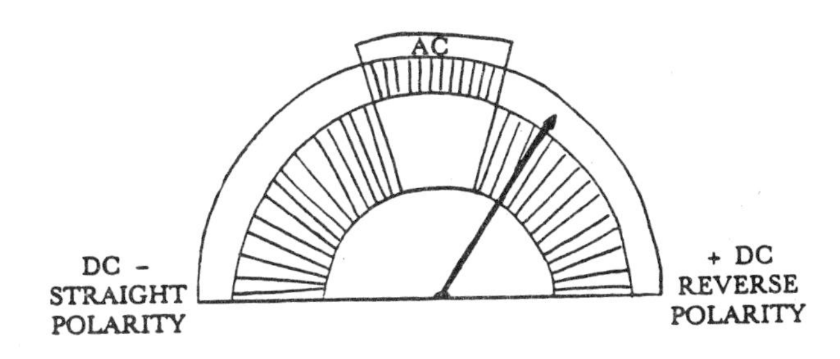

DC REVERSE POLARITY

DC reverse polarity is the kind of current most often used in arc welding. When you use DC reverse polarity, the electrode is hotter than the work piece.

Figure 14

Allied Health was another trade area that contained a number of abstract concepts. A common entry-level job in this area is transportation aide. The job requires that a student master a number of terms that identify specific departments in a hospital, e.g. *audiology department, opthalmology department, cardiology department.* The development of effective illustrations of these concepts proved to be quite difficult and time-consuming. One example, in which the artist was able to design a drawing that seemed to illustrate the concept yet maintain the criteria of "simplicity," was *x-ray department* (Fig. 15).

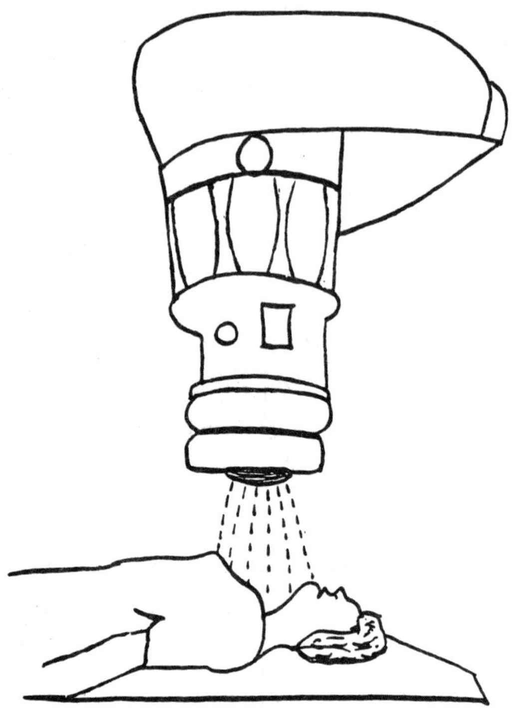

X-RAY DEPARTMENT

The X-ray Department is where x-rays, pictures of the insides of the body, are made.

Figure 15

A term that presented another type of illustration/design problem was *cardiology department*. The illustrator used the common valentine heart to depict the meaning of cardiology. There was some discussion over whether this was not a misrepresentation, since it was not technically accurate. It was decided, however, that the use of the technically accurate picture of the heart organ presumed prior knowledge on the part of learning handicapped and disadvantaged students that was unlikely. Thus, *communication* was considered more important than technical accuracy (Fig. 16).

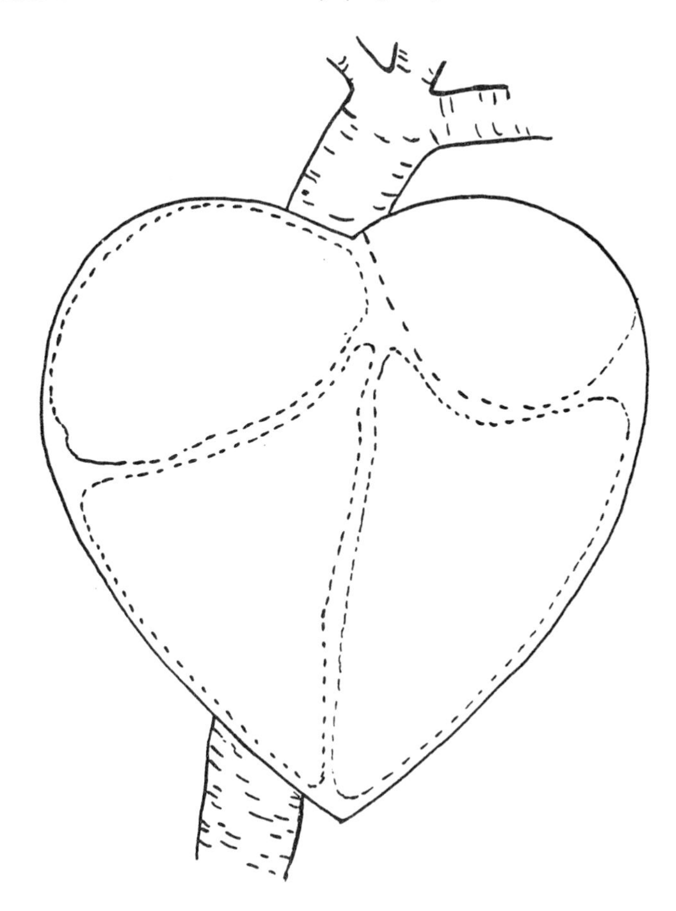

CARDIOLOGY
DEPARTMENT

The Cardiology Department helps people with heart trouble.

Say (*card* ee *all* uh jee dee *part* ment)

Figure 16

Another illustration/design problem was how to represent size concepts. For instance, in Culinary Arts there were a number of terms that required some sort of size discrimination. In the lesson on Cutting, *chop, mince,* and *dice* all refer to cutting procedures. They differ only in the size of the finished products. Our original approach differentiated sizes by categorizing chop as large pieces, dice as medium-sized pieces, and mince as very small pieces. An inherent problem with these descriptions is that small, medium, and large are relative terms; that is, they might mean different things to a 6 foot 2 inch student and to a 5 foot 1 inch student. Thus, we elected to include in the definition that involved size comparisons reference to items with which the students would be familiar (Fig. 17).

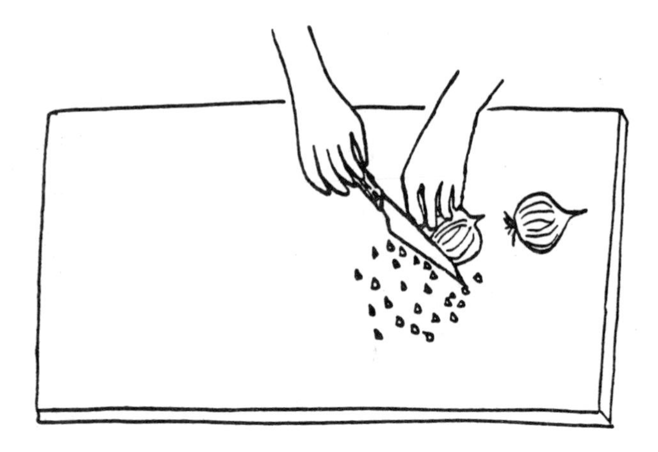

MINCE

To mince means to cut food into very small pieces. The pieces are about as big as a grain of rice.

say (mints)

Figure 17

Another area that required size discrimination in Culinary Arts was the variety of knives. A major distinguishing feature of the different knives is the length of the blades. Since learning handicapped and disadvantaged students frequently have trouble discriminating 4 inches versus 6 inches, an alternate measurement system was needed. Consequently, the length of each knife was defined in relation to a common item rather than in inches. For example:

> A **paring knife** is used to cut skin off fruits and vegetables. The blade of a paring knife is about as long as a new piece of chalk.
>
> A **french knife** is used to slice, chop, mince, and dice. The blade of a french knife is about the size of a long box of tissues.

An example of a teaching booklet page for *boning knife* is shown in Figure 18.

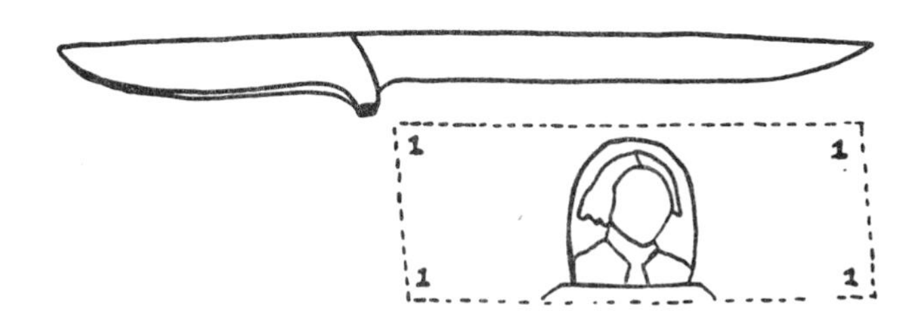

BONING KNIFE

A boning knife is used to remove meat from the bone. The blade of the boning knife is narrow and about as long as a dollar bill.

Figure 18

All the drawings were black and white because the cost of having an illustrator draw in color and the additional expense of duplicating in color were prohibitive. The only area in which this posed a problem was Culinary Arts, a very visually oriented area. Without the use of color, an egg is not a great deal different from a lemon in terms of shape and size. The minor differences in appearance could quite easily be overlooked by a learning handicapped or disadvantaged student. The lack of color as a discimination dimension was also keenly felt in the lesson on sauces, since the most readily discernible difference in the basic sauces is color. We overcame this problem by referring to the color of the sauce in the definition, showing one or two of the major ingredients on the page, and showing the sauce being spooned over a food with which it would normally be served. The definition and illustration of *hollandaise sauce* are shown in Figure 19.

HOLLANDAISE SAUCE

Hollandaise sauce is a yellow egg sauce made from egg yolks, lemon juice, and butter. Hollandaise sauce is put on eggs, vegetables, and fish.

Figure 19

The third type of word that was referred to earlier was the process word. Each of the trade areas had terms that denoted a series of steps. In Culinary Arts, *clarify* means to make clear and is actually a series of steps. In clarifying butter, for instance, (1) you melt the butter, (2) a sediment of salt and other additives drops to the bottom, (3) a foam forms on the top, and (4) clear liquid is left in the middle. You then (5) skim off the foam, (6) drain off the clear liquid, and (7) throw out the sediment.

That this is a multistep process posed problems for developing both the definition and the drawing. Since one of the a priori criteria for instructional package development allowed only one illustration per term, and since learning handicapped and disadvantaged students are easily distracted by too many stimuli, it was essential that the visual image stimulus capture the major concept even though it was not possible to show the entire process. This required numerous drafts to maintain the technical accuracy while at the same time meeting the learning needs of the students.

The definition of a term such as *clarify* also required special attention. The definitions did not attempt to give a detailed description of *how* to perform the process. Definitions were written to focus on the major component of the process and to help the student remember that component. It is incumbent upon the Culinary Arts teacher to show the student *how* to clarify butter.

A further restriction was imposed on the size of the type and the size of the page. All definitions were done in primary type to increase the readability and to help those students who might have visual problems. Only one word, definition, and illustration were put on a half-sized page to avoid the problem of too much stimuli, which was discussed earlier. This meant that the definition was limited to a maximum of seven to eight lines and three to four simple sentences. The illustration and definition of *clarify* are shown in Figure 20.

In summary, the criteria for the definitions and illustrations used in the development of the self-instructional packages were as follows:

1. Fourth grade vocabulary
2. Primary type: three to four simple sentences
3. Half-sized page
4. One line drawing per term
5. Black and white drawings

Development of Additional Learning Aids

In addition to the teaching booklets containing the vocabulary, students also had access to a cassette tape for each lesson. Lessons

CLARIFY

To clarify means to make a liquid clear. To clarify butter, you heat the butter and then take out the cloudy part and keep the clear part.

Figure 20

were put on individual tapes so that students did not have to hunt for the beginning of a lesson on a longer tape. Since approximately 20 percent of the students using the materials had less than a fourth grade reading level, it was felt that the addition of an audiotape would enhance their learning. All of the directions for use of the materials as well as the definitions themselves were recorded on the tape for each lesson. The resource room teachers involved in the study reported that all students were able to use the materials independently after an initial demonstration by the teacher.

The materials also included flash cards, color coded to the booklet covers. The flash cards were heavy poster board and were numbered to correspond to the page numbers in the booklets. After the student had gone through the lesson in the booklet with the tape, the directions guided him to the flash cards. The student then went through the flash cards, checking himself on the definitions after looking at the word and illustration. The materials are self-instructional and are geared for success. If the student did not know all the definitions with the flash cards, he was able to go back to the booklets and review. Only after the student was 100 percent correct on the flash cards was he supposed to go on to the activity for that particular lesson. The activity was also designed as a student aid and was meant to reinforce the concepts learned. The activity sheets contained miniaturized copies of the illustrations in the booklets. They had, essentially, the same structure as the flash cards except that the student now had to match the correct definition and word/illustration. This was also self-paced, and the directions told the student to go back to the booklet and tape if he/she did not get 100 percent on the activity.

Only if the student knew all the flash cards and had gotten all the activity matches correct was he/she instructed to go to the teacher and ask for the checkup for that lesson. The checkup also contained the same miniaturized pictures as the activity sheet, except that the student was now required to make two matches, the word to the picture and the word to the definition.

Field Test Results

The use of the visual image approach to teaching technical language to mildly learning handicapped and disadvantaged students has been validated in three studies. Two of the studies were done with high school age vocational students. The first study was concerned only with graphic arts terminology and used a "picture-dictionary" approach with more than one word/illustration on a page. All twenty-four of the students in this small sample successfully reached the criterion of 100 percent recall (Gardner & Kurtz, 1979b).

The second study involved evaluation of the one picture/one definition per page format presented in this chapter. A total of eighty-seven students from five vocational schools participated. Fifty-two students were learning handicapped (many could have been classified as disadvantaged), and thirty-five regular vocational students served as the comparison group. Both groups were pre- and post-tested on the vocabulary from the specific trade area in which they were enrolled. The learning handicapped/disadvantaged group from all five trade areas made statistically significant gains on the number

ALLIED HEALTH II
Activity 11
Lesson 11

Name______________________________ Date______________

Match the picture and the meaning. Put the right number on the line beside the meaning.

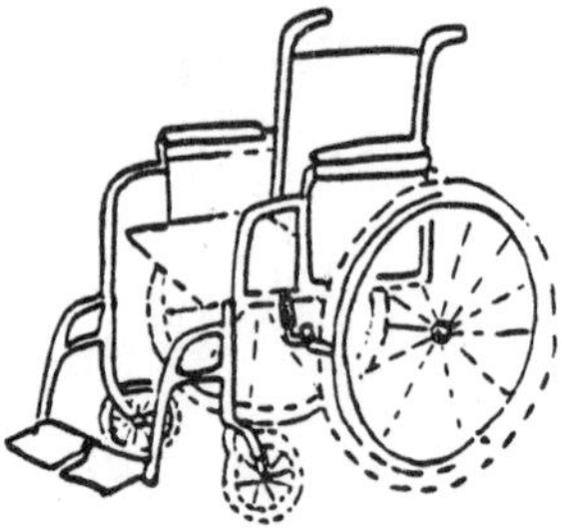

1. wheelchair

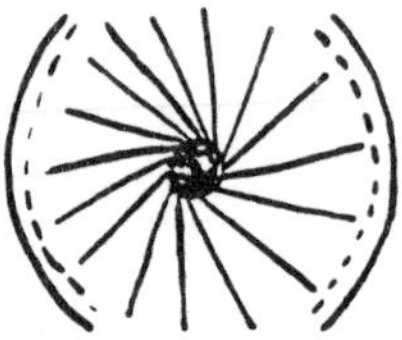

2. spokes

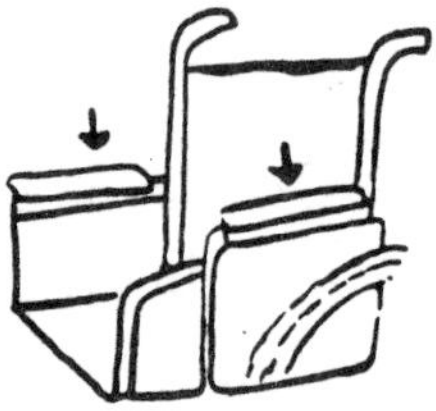

3. armrest

4. footplate

_____ This part of the wheelchair holds up the arms and the upper half of the body.

_____ A flat slat at the bottom of the wheelchair that holds the feet.

_____ Metal rim fastened to the wheel. The patient uses this to move and steer the wheelchair.

_____ Wires that connect the edge of the wheel to the center of the wheel.

CULINARY ARTS I
Checkup 1
Lesson 1

Name____ Date__________________

Put the number of the picture next to the word *AND* next to the meaning. The first one is done for you.

WORD	*PICTURE*	*MEANING*
_____ boning knife		1 _____ Cut lines into meat so spices sink in.
		_____ This machine cuts and slices food.
1 _____ score	1	
		_____ Cut raw meat like steak with this knife.
_____ butcher's knife	2	
		_____ Use this knife to cut meat from bone.
_____ slicing machine	3	
	4	

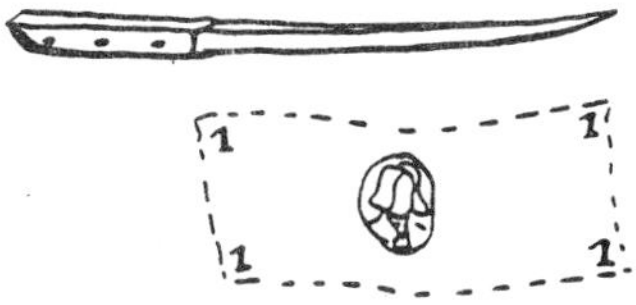

of technical words mastered while the comparison group did not. There were significant differences between the two groups, with most of the learning disabled students achieving 100% mastery and none of the regular students achieving 100% mastery. (Gardner, Beatty, & Warren, 1981.)

In the third study (Avallon, 1980), twenty-four junior high school students classified as mildly handicapped (one or more years below grade level on reading vocabulary) were assigned to three treatment groups for learning twenty generic technical terms. One group studied in the traditional way, memorizing prose definitions. The other two groups used materials based on the vocabulary packages described in this chapter. One of these two groups used an audiotape in addition to the visual image materials. Both of the groups using the visual image materials learned significantly more words than the traditional method group. However, there were no differences between the two visual image groups, suggesting that the use of an audiotape may not be necessary.

In summary, a visual image approach to teaching technical language is a viable way to help learning handicapped and disadvantaged students master essential vocabulary. The process of developing materials may be time-consuming for some teachers, but the effort is well worth it.

REFERENCES

Avallon, J.L. Visual image approaches to teaching technical vocabulary to learning handicapped students. Master's thesis, Boston University, September, 1980.

Brolin, D. *Vocational Preparation of Retarded Citizens*. Columbus, OH: Merrill, 1976.

Dahl, P., Appleby, J. & Lipe, D. *Mainstreaming Guidebook for Vocational Educators*. Salt Lake City, UT: Olympus, 1978.

Gardner, D.C., Beatty, G.J., & Warren, S.A. A visual image approach to teaching entry-level technical terminology to learning handicapped students. *Reading Improvement,* Summer, 1981.

Gardner, D.C., Beatty, G.J., & Warren, S.A. Vocational curriculum modification: Teaching technical language to learning handicapped students. Final Report: Vol. 1, Project HIRE, USOE Grant No. G007701947, Boston, MA: Boston University School of Education, September, 1979. *Resources in Education,* August, 1980, ERIC ED 183 738.

Gardner, D.C., Beatty, G.J., & Warren, S.A. *Words at Work: Graphic Arts*.

Gardner, D.C., Beatty, G.J., & Warren, S.A. *Words at Work: Allied Health* (Contains a teacher's handbook and three student workbooks.)

Gardner, D.C., Beatty, G.J., & Warren, S.A. *Words at Works: Arc Welding* (Contains a teacher's handbook and three student workbooks.)

Gardner, D.C., Beatty, G.J., & Warren, S.A. *Words at Work: Upholstery* (Contains a teacher's handbook and three student workbooks.)

Gardner, D.C., Beatty, G.J., & Warren, S.A. *Words at Work: Culinary Arts* (Contains a teacher's handbook and three student workbooks.)

Gardner, D.C. & Kurtz, M.A. An evaluation of a curriculum model for teaching phototypesetting to handicapped students. *Education 99(3)*:314-320, 1979a.

Gardner, D.C. & Kurtz, M.A. Teaching technical vocabulary to handicapped students. *Reading Improvement,* 61-65, Fall, 1979b.

Redmann, D.H. Vocational reading and math CBTE project. *Florida Vocational Journal,* 14-15, January-February, 1979.

Warren, S.A. Pros and cons of normalization. Paper presented at the Sixth Annual International Symposium on Mental Retardation, University of Vienna, Vienna, Austria, March, 1973.

Wheatley, G. The right hemisphere's role in problem solving. *Arithmetic Teacher, 25*:36-39, 1977.

Wolfensberger, W. *The Principle of Normalization in Human Services.* Toronto, Canada: National Institute on Mental Retardation, York University, 1972.

CHAPTER 4

CURRICULUM MODIFICATION: BEHAVIOR AND ATTITUDES

LAST week Scott's friend Jimmy was fired from his job. This was the fourth time within the last nine months that he had been fired from a job he was capable of doing. Sheila, Jimmy's girlfriend, has a similar history of failure. Neither Sheila nor Jimmy can hold a job for very long. They just cannot seem to get along with their bosses or with fellow workers. Sheila dropped out of school and is enrolled in a local CETA training program for disadvantaged women. Jimmy is enrolled in a cooperative education program in Culinary Arts.

Both Jimmy and Sheila represent the "work personality" types that are often found in the ranks of mildly learning handicapped and disadvantaged youth. They display an observable inability to accept responsibility for their own lives and careers and constantly blame their failings on others. They do not have the personal skills and knowledge necessary to make wise career choices. They lack an understanding of self as related to work and have inappropriate work attitudes. With the unemployment rate for youth estimated to be triple that of the national average (Hoyt et al., 1974), the likelihood of Jimmy and Sheila becoming productive members of our work-oriented society is low. The problem, then, is, How do vocational education teachers, counselors, and special education personnel deal with students like Sheila and Jimmy? How do we help them help themselves? How do we develop strategies that will alter their seemingly unalterable journey towards failure?

One approach that holds out hope is the USOE Career Education model. One of the major tenets of the career education movement is that personal career development for each individual is a lifelong process amenable to educational and counseling intervention throughout that life span (Hoyt, 1975). Thus the challenge to vocational educators and other specialists is to devise ways to alter the process in a positive manner. For our purposes, we are concerned with (1) altering the "work personality," which we define as the behaviors, attitudes, and knowledge that the learning handicapped and disadvantaged adolescent brings to the job and (2) how these affect the student's job performance, career choice, and acceptance of responsibility. Our practical experience and the research that we have been involved in over the years have led us to believe that a large part of the variance in the work personality can be measured and explained from two overlapping theoretical areas: (1) locus of control of personality, as postulated in Rotter's social learning theory (1954), and (2) the concept of career maturity (Crites, 1973), which has its foundation in Super's career development theory (1953).

In recent years there has been considerable research on both of these theoretical approaches. This research shows great promise for vocational educators who are faced with the challenges of developing ways to bring about positive changes in the work personalities of their students. The purpose of this chapter is to provide the reader with a nontechnical overview of the theories, some of the relevant research, and a discussion of how this information can be used by vocational educators, counselors, and other specialists to help students like Jimmy and Sheila make a better adjustment to the work world.

The strategies discussed in this chapter have been tested empirically and have been found to make significant changes in the work personality of students who are handicapped or disadvantaged. Moreover, in most cases, they have been implemented by teachers or counselors who did not have special training.

Accepting Responsibility: Locus of Control

The struggle by vocational teachers and counselors to help students who are learning handicapped or disadvantaged to acquire the skills of a specific occupation and to learn how to get and hold a job is, in many cases, a history of countless setbacks and failures. More often than not, the student, after a track record of failure, just seems to give up. The learning handicapped or disadvantaged vocational student who exhibits this pattern of behavior just does not seem to try as hard while many of his/her peers, some not as intelligent, make it. According to Gardner & Gardner (1973), it may well be that the student

> doesn't try because he [she] doesn't see any point in making the effort

> . . . [He/She] just doesn't believe that there is any connection between . . . successes [or failures] and his [her] own behavior. This phenomenon has been recognized by psychologists and is called locus of control. (P. 41)

Locus of control is one of the postulates of Rotter's social learning theory (Rotter, 1965; 1966; 1975). Locus of control is concerned with a person's belief about the contingencies of one's own behavior. Locus of control refers to the degree to which a person accepts responsibility for the outcomes of his or her own behavior. A vocational student who believes that what happens is a result of his or her own behavior is said to have an internal locus of control. Conversely, a vocational student who believes that what happens is a matter of chance, luck, fate, or the whims of powerful others is said to have an external locus of control.

Within the context of vocational instruction and counseling for preparing mildly learning handicapped and disadvantaged youth for work "this means that persons who are more internal will be more likely to achieve by working harder to meet goals than those who are external" (Gardner and Beatty, 1980a). The concept that persons with an internal locus of control are more productive and serious workers is supported by considerable evidence.

Tseng (1970) reports significant differences on a number of work-related variables between internals and externals enrolled in a vocational rehabilitation program with 140 clients. He found that internals were higher on

> their ability to work with others, cooperation, self reliance, courtesy, reliability, work knowledge, care of equipment, safety practices, compliance with shop rules, training satisfaction, need for achievement, . . . etc. (P. 487)

In another study, which involved disadvantaged trainees in a CETA program, von Esch (1978) found that the trainees who were more internal on locus of control were more likely to be the best performers. These studies, and others, serve to underscore the importance of taking locus of control into consideration when designing work training or counseling programs for mildly learning handicapped and disadvantaged students. Locus of control is not only an important variable in any work training program, it is particularly important when dealing with handicapped and disadvantaged vocational students, especially those who appear to be ready to join the ranks of the chronically underemployed or unemployed. As Lefcourt (1966) points out:

> . . . groups whose social position is one of minimal power either by class or race (or handicap) tend to score higher in the *external* control direction. Within racial groupings, class interacts so that the double handicap of lower-class and "lower caste" seems to produce persons with the highest expectancy of external control. (P. 212)

Thus, the many stumbling blocks to successful vocational training and employment associated with low economic status and/or handicaps are further confounded by the tendency for handicapped and disadvantaged youth to be more external in their locus of control orientation (Gardner & Beatty, 1980a).

Fortunately, the situation for Jimmy and Sheila is not as bleak as the research indicates. Although handicapped and disadvantaged persons as a group tend to be more external and less achievement oriented than their middle-class peers, it need not be thought of as a permanent, fixed condition. Locus of control orientation is learned behavior and has been found to be amenable to remediation. Because it is based on social learning, it is possible to change a person's locus of control from external to internal.

There is a growing body of research in this area that suggests that locus of control can be altered in the internal direction for both youths and adults. One very effective approach for helping persons become more internal is the integration of certain locus of control change techniques in a life planning/life skills/career development model (Beatty & Gardner, 1979; Bigelow, in review; Curry, 1980; Gardner, Beatty & Bigelow, 1981). Moreover, the same strategies used by these researchers have shown that when you change a person's locus of control, you can simultaneously change the level of the person's career maturity. Before discussing the actual methods used to change locus of control of learning handicapped and disadvantaged vocational students, let's look at career maturity and its relationship to work attitudes.

Career Maturity

One of the important assumptions of career development is that it is an ongoing lifelong process. According to Donald Super, a major theorist in the field, career development is essentially a process of developing and implementing the self-concept. In fact, Super says that your choice of an occupation is the implementation of your self-concept. Modern career education programs are based on the assumption that the career development of individual students can be altered or modified through various educational and counseling strategies.

Another theorist in the field, J.O. Crites, has developed an inventory to measure a person's career maturity on a number of dimensions. The Crites Career Maturity Inventory (1973) has six different subscales that respectively measure attitudes, knowing yourself, knowing about jobs, ability to make choices about jobs, planning, and decision making. These essential skills and attitudes are keystones to successful employment and training.

While there is not as much empirical data available on career maturity change techniques as there is on locus of control change techniques, there are a number of studies that suggest that the work personality of a student is directly related to locus of control and career maturity. Cowan (1979) has theorized that

> one can deduce from social learning theory and career development theory that the process of learning to set career related goals will not only heighten the expectancy that the goals will be achieved . . . (helping the person to become more internal) . . . but will also lead to increased career maturity. (P. 13)

A careful analysis of the theoretical postulates of career development theory (Crites, 1973) and social learning theory (Rotter, 1966) logically leads to the hypothesis of a significant relationship between the two variables. If this relationship exists, then the vocational student who is more career mature would axiomatically be more internal on locus of control. There is a growing body of research that shows this to be, in fact, a supportable hypothesis (see Appendix A).

A Work Personality Development Model

Recent research has shown that many of the same techniques used to modify a person's locus of control, either in a counseling program or an instructional program, have also been successful in simultaneously helping the same student to become more career mature. This section of the book offers a twofold model (see Fig. 21) for developing instructional and/or counseling programs to accomplish positive changes in the work personality of vocational students like Jimmy and Sheila. The techniques are derived from numerous studies that have been effective in changing locus of control of students and clients in various settings. In some instances, these same techniques have been shown to change both locus of control and career maturity (Curry, 1980; Beatty, Gardner & Bigelow, 1981; Bigelow, 1981).

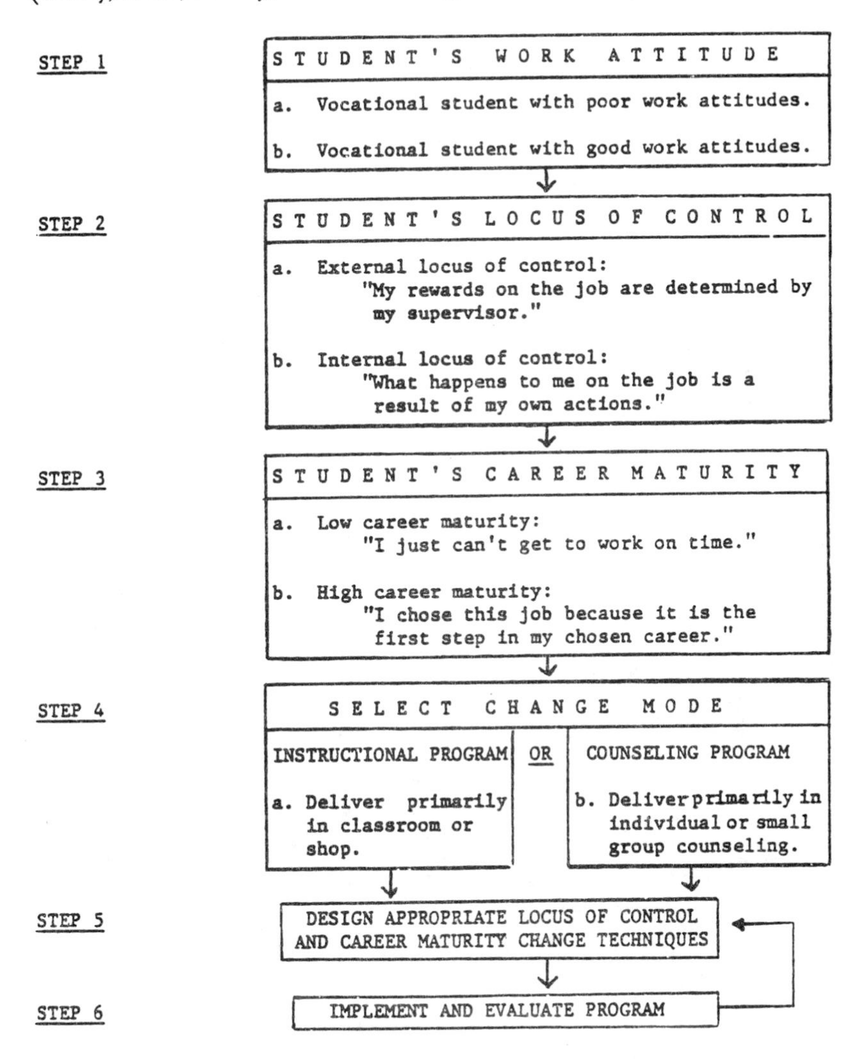

Figure 21. Work personality change techniques model.

Work Personality Change Techniques

As we mentioned earlier, the strategies for implementing changes in a mildly learning handicapped or disadvantaged vocational student are derived from both career development theory (Super, 1953; Crites, 1974) and Rotter's social learning theory (1954; 1966; 1975). In addition, the strategies discussed below are all based on empirically validated procedures. Some of the strategies are primarily oriented towards changing a person's locus of control orientation from external to internal. Others focus on both locus of control as well as student's level of career maturity. Those strategies which have an impact on both career maturity and locus of control have an asterisk (*). Those without asterisks are exclusively locus of control change techniques.

It should be noted that the purpose of separating students into those who are external on locus of control and low in career maturity and into those who are internal on locus of control and high in career maturity is for purposes of evaluation only. In the actual delivery of the counseling and/or instruction it is not necessary to separate students into these groupings. The reason for this is that both locus of control orientation and level of career maturity are alterable variables; that is, they are learned behavior and can be modified. Thus, if a student already exhibits high career maturity and internal locus of control, the strategies used to change a student from external to internal and from low to high career maturity will at the same time reinforce the internal locus of control orientation and high career maturity of the students who exhibit these behaviors. In other words, the student who already has an appropriate set of work attitudes will be reinforced in maintaining them by the change techniques employed to change the work attitudes of vocational students who do not have good work attitudes.

The strategies for designing counseling and supervision procedures for helping mildly learning handicapped and disadvantaged vocational students develop a more appropriate work personality are discussed below. In addition, there are procedures to be used in designing classroom or shop strategies. However, there is a natural overlap between the counseling strategies and the instructional strategies presented in the following two sections. We have arbitrarily divided the techniques into two sections for clarity of discussion only.

Instructional Strategies

Change Technique 1: REWARD RESPONSIBLE BEHAVIORS IMMEDIATELY

As you can easily see, this procedure makes sense. If a vocational student displays self-initiative or takes charge of the situation on his own, you reinforce this behavior immediately. Sometimes, just a word of praise is sufficient. Suppose that Mary is working on a dangerous piece of equipment and she notices that the safety guard next to the blade is loose. On her own she shuts down the machine, finds a screwdriver, and repairs the equipment. It is at this point that you should find the time to praise her for accepting responsibility for safety. Similarly, suppose that Scott, while working the counter in the school restaurant, notices that the cashier is overwhelmed with a long line of customers. He moves to the second cash register without being directed to do so and proceeds to help some of the customers. This is an excellent opportunity for the vocational teacher or supervisor to take time to praise Scott. While these examples may seem self-evident, in reality we all tend to forget to focus on the positive. Had Scott or Mary not made such a move, the chances are that many supervisors would have given a direct order (reinforcing the "powerful other" syndrome) and used a negative tone. Remember, the accent here is to focus on the positive desirable behaviors and to point out to the student the rewards for acting responsibly. One of the advantages of using positive reinforcement, of course, is that while you have to start out using it regularly, once you have consistently applied it over time you can begin to use an intermittent schedule of reinforcement. That is, once the responsible behaviors appear to be solidified, you can reinforce them only occasionally and maintain the behaviors. Conversely, if you use negative reinforcement you have to use it constantly for it to be effective.

Change Technique 2: HOLD DISCUSSIONS EXPLAINING LOCUS OF CONTROL

This is one of the most powerful locus of control change techniques. Simply explain to a group of vocational students that persons who believe that what happens to them is a result of their own actions usually do better in shop and on the job than those students who always blame their problems on the teacher or supervisor. Make a point of being frank about the concept of locus of control and do so using the student's own vocabulary. Hold frequent discussions with the class whenever the opportunity presents itself.

Change Technique 3: TEACH GOAL SETTING*

Teaching vocational students to set goals is a powerful technique for helping mildly learning handicapped and disadvantaged students to become more internal on locus of control. Concurrently, this technique also produces positive changes in the level of the student's career maturity. There is extensive literature on the positive effects of instituting goal-setting behaviors on the performance of individuals. The payoff for teaching goal setting to students is multifaceted. It will not only affect their locus of control and career maturity positively (e.g. Curry, 1980; Bigelow, 1981; Gardner, Beatty & Bigelow, 1981; Beatty & Gardner, 1979) but will also effect changes in work performance (Gardner, 1974; Kliebhan, 1967) and academic performance (Gardner & Gardner, 1979; Warner & De Jung, 1969). Goal-setting techniques lend themselves to both individual and group instruction. For instance, you may involve the class in developing a set of objectives for a class project involving the construction of a tool shed or the preparation of a banquet for a school social group. In either case, all students would be expected to participate in the development of the project objectives, the determination of appropriate strategies and timelines to meet these objectives, the development of individual project member's goals and timelines, and the selection of appropriate guidelines for evaluating outcomes both of the group and the individual.

For goal setting to effect positive changes in career maturity, one should also emphasize the relationship between job-related goals and short- and long-term career goals. Goal setting can also be used individually with students. You can institute a practice of having students periodically set personal performance goals and work with you in establishing methods of evaluation of the achievement of the goals. Goal setting on an individual basis should also involve discussions of how these goals are important to the student's achievement of his or her career goals.

Change Technique 4: PROVIDE OPPORTUNITIES FOR THE STUDENT TO ASSUME RESPONSIBILITY

Change technique sections with an * indicate the technique is effective in changing both locus of control and career maturity.

Try to provide opportunities for each student to assume, at a moderately increasing rate, responsibility for both the quality and quantity of her or his production whenever possible. In the beginning this will involve close supervision and structured activities. As the student begins to display responsible behaviors, supervision and structure can gradually be "faded" towards independent functioning. At every opportunity, point out to the student the connection between rewards (grades, money, privileges, praise, etc.) and the quantity and quality of the production.

Change Technique 5: DISCUSS FREQUENTLY THE CONNECTION BETWEEN REWARDS AND PERFORMANCE

This technique has been around for a long time. In human services we sometimes forget that rewards (money, raises, promotion, etc.) are ultimately tied to the quality and quantity of one's own work production. This technique can be combined with the strategies for implementing Change Technique 4. Plan a schedule of class discussions, individual performance evaluations, and readings about persons who have achieved into your annual plan. The point is to take every opportunity deliberately to point out to your students the basic connection between rewards and personal efforts and performance. One good way to do this is to keep a performance chart on the wall with weekly recording of individual achievements. In some programs this has been coupled with employee or trainee of the week awards.

Change Technique 6: INVOLVE THE STUDENT IN DECISION MAKING AND PLANNING*

One basic characteristic of a career mature person is the ability to make decisions on the job and to plan ahead both for job task completion and for long-term career growth. Try to design your program so that students have ample opportunity to make decisions about their work schedule and career growth and provide periodic sessions where students get involved in planning short- and long-term activities. A good method for introducing decision-making and planning activities is to develop (or purchase) case study materials where job-related problems are presented and students are required to discuss with each other possible solutions to the problems. Case studies on job choice and planning can also be helpful in reinforcing both career maturity and locus of control.

Counseling Strategies

Change Technique 7: PRAISE INTERNAL STATEMENTS*

Be on the lookout for statements from your students that indicate an internal approach to problem solving and praise them. For instance, when Scott or Mary says, "It was my fault, I wasn't planning ahead" or "I will figure it out myself," immediately give an indication of your approval. You might say, in response to the two statements above, "Terrific, it is your responsibility" and "I'm really pleased that you feel confident enough to do it yourself; on the job that's what a good worker does."

Change Technique 8: CONFRONT EXTERNAL STATEMENTS

Take a *positive* approach and confront the external statements of your students. Help them find an internal statement as a substitute. Learning the verbal mediators of "internality" is an essential component for the development of an appropriate work personality. Be on the lookout for external statements, challenge them, and help the student to rephrase the statement towards an internal orientation. By doing this, you will help the student change his or her expectancy for control.

A teacher or counselor who is aware of the negative impact of external statements can do much to help the student become aware of what he or she is really saying. Take a look at the following examples of external statements you might typically hear from students. Examples of challenging comments are included for the first couple of external statements. Think about how you would confront the remaining statements.

Student: "I'm late because my mother didn't wake me up in time."

Teacher/Counselor: "*Whose* responsibility is it to get to school on time, yours or your mother's? What can you do tomorrow to make sure you get up in time?"

Student: "I wasn't in school the other day and nobody told me that we had to do that assignment?"

Teacher/Counselor: "Why is it your friend's responsibility to see that you get the homework? What will you do to check on assignments if you are out again?"

Student: "Boy was I lucky to get an A on that project."

Student: "They made me do it"

Student: "What did you give me for a grade?"

Typical of many disadvantaged and mildly learning handicapped students is the proverbial "They . . ." "They" are responsible (the powerful others) for all my failures and problems. The next time you hear a student blame something on someone else challenge the statement. Say, "What do you mean 'they'? Nobody can make you do anything short of holding a gun to your head. You chose to do that. Why did you choose to do it? What could you have done differently? What will you do next time when a similar thing happens?" etc. The point here is to help the student come to the realization that he or she is always responsible for his or her choices in life. Once students begin to recognize this, they will begin to think through the alternative courses open to them when confronted with a problem. They may not always choose the correct solutions, but they will be their *own* solutions and not those of the nebulous "they" in their lives.

Change Technique 9: FOCUS ON THE HERE AND NOW*

In discussions with the students, focus on the here and now at all times. Don't let them drift back into the "past" as an explanation for avoiding a current problem. Ask, "What can you do now?" to solve this problem. The future is similarly irrelevant. The time is *now* to help the student solve the problem. Typical student response is "I've always been late." Your response should be "What can you do about it *now*?"

Change Technique 10: HAVE STUDENT LIST PERSONAL PROBLEMS AND VERBALIZE SOLUTIONS.

Arrange for the student to list personal problems and have him or her verbalize solutions. A good time to do this is when a student displays external behaviors. A work-related example concerns an employee who could be classified as mildly learning handicapped or disadvantaged. When she managed to get to the office, she was a productive worker, but she often was late or stayed out sick. Her supervisor began to have short discussions with her about the reasons for her behavior, explaining that blaming her lateness and inability to get up in the morning on her husband was "copping out." It soon became clear to her that her husband did not *make* her stay up and watch the late show but rather she chose to do so. The supervisor put a lot of emphasis on the *decision making* necessary for a solution to her daily problems. She began to see that she had the choice of setting her own alarm and the decision of whether or not to stay up late with her husband, who worked different hours. Considerable time was spent explaining the concept of locus of control to her in her own language, helping her verbalize her own solutions to problems and helping her make her own decisions about alternative courses and strategies for solving the problems facing her here and now. She began to see that she looked at her husband (and other relatives) as "powerful others," and therefore they were easily able to manipulate her into doing things she really didn't want to do. Eventually her behavior became more acceptable, and she came to work on time and rarely stayed out "sick." One day she mentioned that she was feeling better now that she was getting more sleep. Not only did she begin to exhibit an internal approach to solving her own personal problems, but she also began to display evidence of a more career mature attitude. She began to see that her job was not what she wanted and that it did not challenge her or meet her interests. She began to seek information on career options and eventually left (with adequate notice) for a more promising career.

Change Technique 11: USE THE LANGUAGE OF RESPONSIBILITY

Always use language that focuses on the acceptance of responsibility for the outcomes of one's own behavior. Don't let your student off the hook. Don't accept excuses. The ideal student is one who says, "I didn't get my act together. It's my fault the project or paper is late. I will have it for you on Monday." Reward this type of approach. Conversely, when a student arrives with a set of excuses such as "I forgot" or "I left it at home" or "My mother . . .," confront these statements positively until the student expresses responsibility for what happened or didn't happen. Help the student verbalize a more internal rationale coupled with strategies for remedying the situation. We repeat, Don't let the student off the hook.

REFERENCES

Arrangio, J. The effects of individual goal-setting conferences and classrooms instruction in human relations on locus of control, school attendance and alienation of disadvantaged high school students. Unpublished doctoral dissertation, Boston University, 1980.

Beatty, G.J. & Gardner, D.C. Goal setting and resume writing as a locus of control change technique with college women. *College Student Journal, 13(1):*315-318, 1979.

Bigelow, E.A. The effects of consumer education and decision-making skill instruction on locus of control orientation and career maturity of high school seniors. Unpublished doctoral dissertation, Boston University, 1981.

Bigelow, E.A. Locus of control, career maturity and economic understanding. In review.

Cowan, G.J. The effects of teaching goal-setting procedures on the career maturity and classroom performance of business college women differing in locus of control. Unpublished doctoral dissertation, Boston University, 1979.

Crites, J.O. *Theory and Research Handbook for the Career Maturity Inventory.* Monterey, CA: CTB/McGraw-Hill, 1973.

Curry, J.A. The effects of life planning instruction and career counseling on locus of control orientation and career maturity scores of university compensatory education students. Unpublished doctoral dissertation, Boston University, 1980.

Dwyer, K. The effects of decision-making and life planning instruction on locus of control orientation, career maturity, and self-concept of disadvantaged adults. Unpublished doctoral dissertation, Boston University, 1981.

Gardner, D.C. Career maturity and locus of control: Important factors in career training. *College Student Journal, 15(3),* Fall, 1981.

Gardner, D.C. Goal setting, locus of control, and work performance of mentally retarded adults. Unpublished doctoral dissertation, Boston University, 1974.

Gardner, D.C. & Beatty, G.J. Locus of control change techniques: Important variables in work training. *Education, 100(3):*237-242, Spring, 1980a.

Gardner, D.C. & Beatty, G.J. Personality characteristics and learning styles of disadvantaged youth: Important considerations in teaching job related language and developing work attitudes. Paper presented at the Leadership Training Institute on CETA/Vocational Education, Special Education and Vocational Rehabilitation Linkages. Hartford, CT: Sheraton-Hartford Hotel, May 4-6, 1980b.

Gardner D.C., Beatty G.J. & Bigelow, E.A. An evaluation of a career development seminar for high school students. In review.

Gardner, D.C., Beatty, G.J., & Bigelow, E.A. Locus of control and career maturity: A pilot evaluation of a life-planning and career development program for high school students. *Adolescence, XVI(63),* Fall, 1981.

Gardner, D.C. & Gardner, P.L. Goal-setting and learning in the high school resource room. *Adolescence, 18(51):*489-493, 1974.

Gardner, D.C. & Gardner, P.L. Locus of control as related to learning effectiveness. *Reading Improvement, 11(2):*41-42, 1974.

Gardner, D.C. & Warren, S.A. *Careers and Disabilities: A Career Education Approach.* Stamford, CT: Greylock Pubs, 1978.

Hoyt, K.B. *An Introduction to Career Education.* U.S. Department of Health, Education, and Welfare Publication No. (OE) 75-00504. Washington, D.C.: U.S. Govt. Print. Office, 1975.

Hoyt, K.B., Evans, R.N., Mackin, E.F. & Mangum, G.L. *Career Education: What It Is and How To Do It.* Salt Lake City, UT: Olympus, 1974.

Kliebhan, J.M. Effects of goal-setting and modeling on job performance of retarded adolescents. *American Journal of Mental Deficiency, 72:*220-226, 1967.

Lefcourt, H.M. Internal vs. external control of reinforcement: A review. *Psychological Bulletin, 66(4):*206-220, 1966.

Rotter, J.B. Generalized expectancies for internal versus external control of reinforcement. *Psychological Monographs, 80* (1, whole No. 609),1966.

Rotter, J.B. *Social Learning and Clinical Psychology.* Englewood Cliffs, NJ: Prentice-Hall, 1954.

Rotter, J.B. Some problems and misconceptions related to the construction of internal vs. external control of reinforcement. *Journal of Consulting and Clinical Psychology, 43(1):*56-67, 1975.

Super, D.E. A theory of vocational development. *American Psychologist, 8(4):*185-190, 1953.

Tseng, M.S. Locus of control as a determinant of job proficiency, employability, and training satisfaction of vocational rehabilitation clients. *Journal of Counseling Psychology, 17(6):*487-491, 1970.

von Esch, P. An inquiry into the effects of a syncretic application of locus of control change techniques to a manpower training program for the economically disadvantaged. Unpublished doctoral dissertation, Boston University, 1978.

Warner, D.A. and De Jung, J.E. *Goal Setting Behavior as an Independent Variable Related to the Performance of Educable Mentally Retarded Male Adolescents on Educational Tasks of Varying Difficulty: Final Report.* Washington, D.C.: U.S. Dept. of Health, Education, and Welfare, Project No. 7-1-115, 1969.

CHAPTER 5

CURRICULUM MODIFICATION: MANAGING CURRICULUM CHANGE

THE MANAGEMENT SYSTEM IN PERSPECTIVE

OVER the past decade there have been some profound changes in the way educators approach the preparation and training of mildly learning handicapped and disadvantaged students for the world of work. These changes have come about as the result of the efforts of many parents, employers, educators, judges, legislators, and other interested groups. The sum of the changes can be described by the term *normalization* of the mildly handicapped and disadvantaged. That is, the intent of all those concerned with the welfare, growth, and development of these special populations is to *increase the probability that a learning handicapped and disadvantaged individual can lead a normal life* consonant with his or her own abilities and interests.

It is obvious to all of us who are concerned with the Scotts of this world that learning handicapped and disadvantaged children will *no longer* be serviced in special programs or special classes but instead will attend regular school programs (Brenton, 1977). The implications of the current trends and accompanying legislation concerning the career/vocational education for these special populations are readily discernible in the recent expenditures (and priorities related thereto) of federal and state monies.

The management system presented herein is a reflection of the authors' response to this incredibly complex problem. Since educational problems are not univariate but multivariate in nature, there is no simple way to accomplish the goal of normalization, including mainstreaming. A complete treatise on the subject of managing a comprehensive normalization program for these students is beyond the scope of this book. Nevertheless, we have identified from the literature and our own experience one area that seems critical to the success or failure of the Scotts in our society in career/vocational programs: the development of a systematic way to modify the curriculum to accommodate the special learning needs of mildly learning handicapped and disadvantaged students enrolled in skill-training programs. In our work with many school systems, the underlying curriculum modification problem for this group is almost universally one of determining how to provide support instruction (and develop appropriate materials) for teaching the *academics* of the specific occupational area. That is, learning handicapped and academically disadvantaged students have disproportionate problems mastering the technical language and technical math of the particular trade they are studying. The management system for curriculum change discussed herein will therefore focus on a description of *one* way to develop new curriculum materials to be used to support the "academics" of specific trade areas. The examples are from our own experience in dealing with technical vocabulary (see Chapter 3). The point of the discussion in this chapter is not to demonstrate how one can develop quality curriculum support materials for teaching technical vocabulary but rather to illustrate a management process that has equal application to the modification and development of curricula in any topic area that will enhance the vocational training of these special populations.

SUPPORT MODELS IN PERSPECTIVE. Before describing the management system for curriculum change, it seems appropriate to discuss briefly the typical programs for dealing with mildly learning handicapped and disadvantaged youth in career/vocational education. Figures 22 and 23 illustrate ideal "models." For the midly learning handicapped the process includes an initial referral and career/vocational assessment period, the development of an IEP/IVEP (see Chapter 7), and an implementation stage. The implementation stage may include resource room support services in basic academics related to high school graduation requirements, the academics of the specific trade (related instruction), mainstreaming into the regular program, career counseling, work study and cooperative education experiences, and final job placement and follow-up. In most instances, the resource room support services should include the use of specially modified curriculum materials to assist the student in learning the "academics" of the particular vocational program as well as consulting services to the vocational teacher by the resource room teacher. In our experience, it is rare that all of these activities are provided. One weak link has been making provisions for the acquisition of materials or the development of modified materials. Thus, our management system is geared to this area.

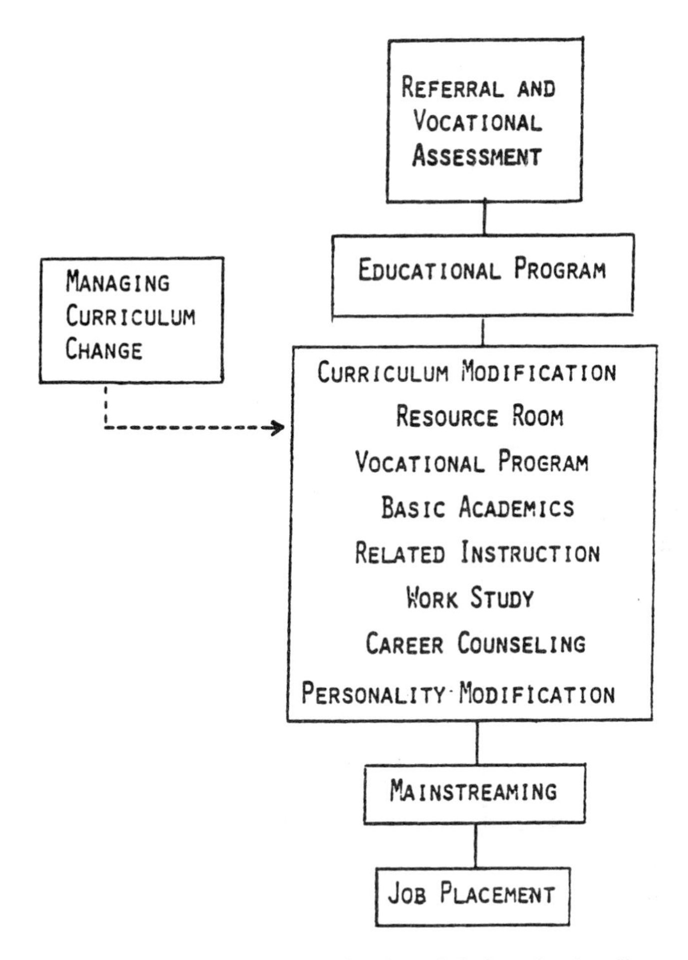

Figure 22. Vocational education for the mildly learning handicapped.

For the disadvantaged student, the "ideal" system of services is similar to that for the mildly learning handicapped. Usually, however, the supportive services are remedial, e.g. visits to a reading teacher, are usually less comprehensive since IVEPs are not required, and rarely occur in a formal resource room. As mentioned earlier, it is our contention that the same services provided the learning handicapped should be provided to the academically disadvantaged student, that is, a more comprehensive assessment resulting in a specific, individualized program of instruction, e.g. an IVEP system.

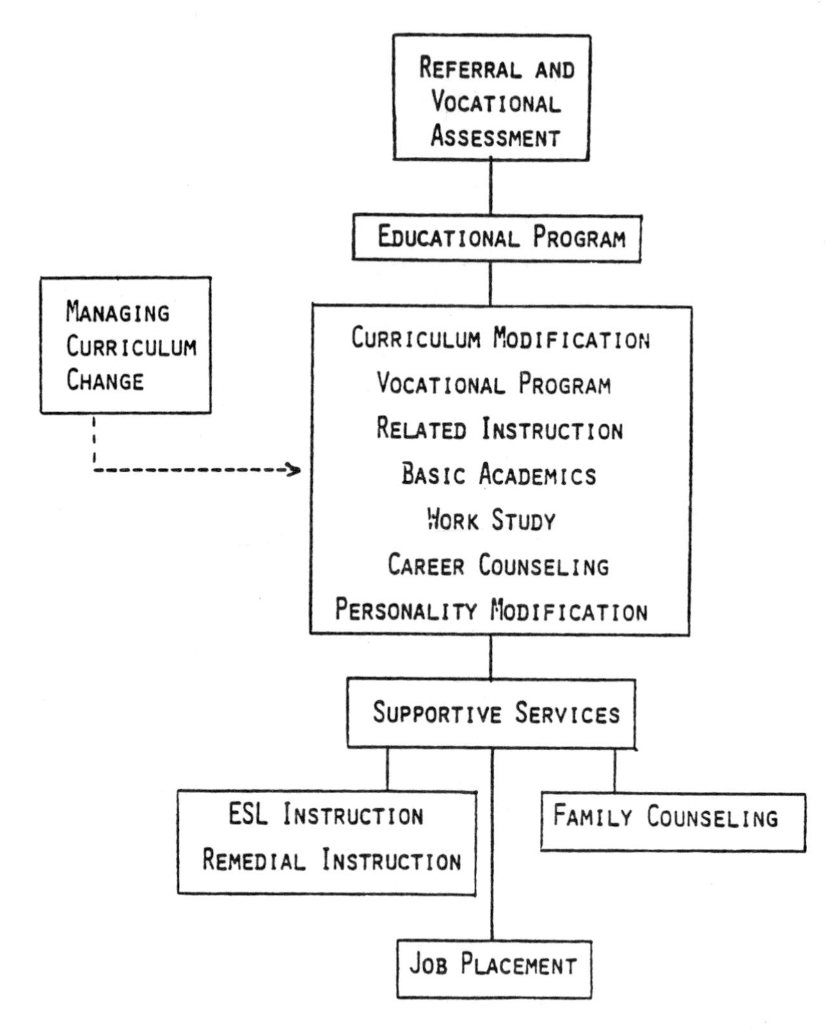

Figure 23. Vocational education for the disadvantaged.

Within the context of the ideal service delivery models for mildly learning handicapped and disadvantaged students enrolled in vocational training programs, the management model illustrated in this chapter will focus on two problems: (1) how to manage curriculum change, and (2) specifically how to modify the vocational curriculum to meet the needs of these special populations by developing support materials (self-instructional packages) to teach the academics of the trade area.

OVERVIEW OF CHAPTER 5

This chapter describes and critiques an illustrative management system that has been field-tested (Gardner & Beatty, 1979; Gardner & Kurtz, 1977) and that is designed to develop supplementary vocational curriculum materials (self-instructional packages) for use by support personnel to assist mildly learning handicapped and disadvantaged students to master the entry-level technical vocabulary of specific trade areas. The management model is product development oriented, using interdisciplinary teams of teachers, administrators, and university personnel to solve practical problems. A standards/strategies paradigm was used in this model for curriculum development. Some of the responses to solving the standards/strategies approach came from previous experience, others from the literature on curriculum development, and some from clinical hunches. According to Borgen and Davis (1971), there are three models or strategies under which most vocational curriculum development work can be categorized: (1) Tylerian models; (2) systems models; and (3) product development models. Our management system can be loosely categorized as *product development oriented.* However, elements from the other approaches are incorporated. Within the context of our product development orientation, the team approach forms the keystone of our management process. A description of the procedures used to develop vocational curriculum materials (self-instructional packages) in the form of a standards/strategies paradigm constitutes the management systems offered in this chapter.

THE STANDARDS/STRATEGIES PARADIGM. The management model presented herein, to reiterate, is product development oriented. Much of the model was derived from practical experience of the authors in industry and education. Thus the foundation for our model is primarily derived from practical experience in managing projects, supplemented by empirically derived data from the literature and clinical hunches. Much of the basic approach is from the industrial experience of the senior author, that is, goal directed and product oriented.

The importance of goal direction in management is exemplified by a multitude of works on management by objectives and by an extensive body of research conducted on a level of aspiration by psychologists and educators over the past fifty years (e.g. Fryer, 1964). Moreover, there is considerable evidence that teachers prefer to work with management personnel in task-oriented situations having tangible outcomes (Tanner & Tanner, 1975).

The standards/strategies paradigm management model is illustrated in Figure 24. As illustrated in the figure, the management approach is based on the establishment of nine standards, making the assumption that each of these standards is a prerequisite to the de-

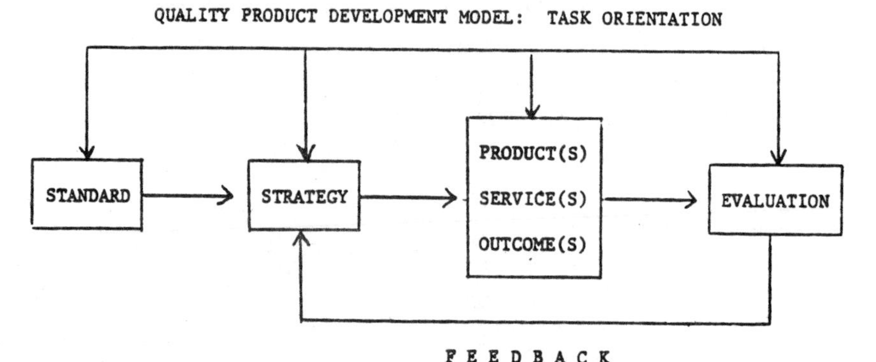

Figure 24. Standards/strategy paradigm

velopment of quality products. For each of the standards, a strategy or several strategies have been formulated. It is hypothesized that each of the strategies would lead to the development of a product, service, or other outcome. This approach, while designed and field-tested in the development of quality curriculum materials in teaching technical vocabulary, has equal application to other curriculum areas. One can envision this process being used to develop self-instructional packages for teaching technical mathematics, for instance.

STANDARD	STRATEGY	OUTCOME/PRODUCTS
1. Implementation of a system to motivate teacher participants.	Provide a schedule of financial rewards, usable products, public credit and attribution for work.	Adherence to schedules; quality products produced.
2. Implementation of a system to involve key decision makers from schools.	Select an administrator to serve on each school team. Provide a schedule of financial rewards,	Adherence to schedules; relatively smooth process.

	usable products for programs, public credit for program, and attribution of administrator's work.	
3. Use of learning theory and research findings as the basis for materials design.	University specialists analyze curriculum content, design basic teaching strategies and materials format in consultation with curriculum teams.	Field-tested procedures and materials.
4. Selection of content to meet greatest need of students and job market.	Identification of job prospects for students related to trade area selected for development. Teacher identification of student's problem area.	List of terms related to trade areas with good or high employment potential. Job descriptions for teachers. Students with problems. served.
5. Content related to entry-level jobs and frequency of usage.	Employer validation of terms of usage and as entry-level. Professional evaluation of vocabulary coverage.	Validated list of terms.
6. Interdisciplinary curriculum development approach. Both resource room and vocational education instructors provide input into curricular planning.	Small, in-school team approach.	Instructional materials for use in vocational support system (resource room or special sessions by regular teachers). Increased interdisciplinary cooperation.
7. University management and coordination of interdisciplinary teams in the curriculum development process.	Project activities coordinated by university staff, i.e. planning, evaluation, design and implementation, data analysis, final product writing, etc. Verified at school level.	Product evaluation, curriculum products dissemination.
8. Professional evaluation of products.	University psychologist helps project management develop a practical forma-	Evaluation report.

	tive/summative evaluation design.	
9. Development of teachers' manuals which contain criterion referenced tests and measurable outcomes.	Construction of tests/ behavioral outcomes by project management in consultation with project psychologist.	Teachers' manuals with criterion referenced tests and generic behavioral outcomes for each trade area.

DEFINITION OF TERMS

Management. The definitions of *management* are probably endless. One alternative definition, "judicious use of means to accomplish an end," has been used to formulate our own definition, within the context of managing curriculum development projects: the steps one must take in order to accomplish the goal of curriculum product development.

Curriculum. Even a cursory review of texts in curriculum theory and development reveals a plethora of definitions of *curriculum.* Within the context of career and vocational curriculum development, Gardner & Warren (1978) point out that definitions range from a narrow one that defines curriculum in terms of materials and textbooks to a broad definition that includes every learning experience of the child. Gardner & Warren define curriculum in the context of career/vocational education as

> any experiences which are-planned by and implemented by the school to help children meet specific learning outcomes which have been deduced from the philosophy and goals for the school. Experiences do not have to take place in the classroom or on school property. (P. 113)

Curriculum Modification. Curriculum modification in this chapter refers to the experiences and materials developed and planned by any instructional program to meet the goal of helping the participating mildly learning handicapped and disadvantaged students in the school master the entry-level skills of specific occupations.

Standard. Definitions of the term *standard* range from "the personal flag of the head of state" to "the basis of value in a monetary system." For our purposes, standard refers to the gauge/yardstick that we propose to use as a model or guiding principle in the curriculum development process. Standards should be established a priori as given assumptions of what is needed to produce quality curriculum products. For example, we decided a priori that one prerequisite to curriculum development in vocational education of mildly learning handicapped and disadvantaged students is the provision of appropriate incentives for participating teachers. In response to varying degrees of enthusiasm and cooperation from participating teachers, all of whom were paid the same amount, this standard was studied in more depth to determine other incentives that could be used in future curriculum development and training projects (Gardner & Beatty, 1980).

Strategy. The term *strategy* is derived from the Greek word for "generalship" and in military jargon is concerned with the science and art of military command. An alternative definition is a "careful plan." For project purposes, we defined strategy as the method or plan we used to meet the standards we established for a curriculum development project.

PLAN OF THE CHAPTER

Except for the introductory sections above, each section of the chapter is concerned with at least one or more of the nine standards/strategies used in the development of the illustrative materials described in Chapter 3. While each of the following sections may vary somewhat, the general format consists of the following:

1. Introduction and background of the standard(s)/strategy(ies) under discussion.
2. A description of what we did in addressing the specific problems related to the standard/strategy.
3. A description of the research methods used, if any, to evaluate the management approach.
4. Results of the implementation process and discussion.

WHAT MOTIVATES TEACHERS TO PARTICIPATE?

Background

As any practical manager in education, government, or industry will tell you, the best planned organization chart for a project, unit, department, or division is superfluous if the people in the slots are not cooperative or productive. In planning the field-testing of our management approach to curriculum development a number of assumptions were made about what would motivate the teachers to participate and how they would be selected. These assumptions were largely made on the basis of past experience with similar groups. Also decisions about implementation were limited by the time and budget constraints of a *product development oriented* project.

The team approach has been used in many previous projects and seemed to be the most effective way to ensure content and design inputs from appropriate personnel. While the inputs and production rates of the teams in the other projects varied from school to school, we felt that our new set of incentives and selection process might improve cooperation. The selection process was determined by each school administrator in a very practical way. Each administrator was asked to pick two resource room teachers and two teachers from a trade area to form a team. (This was not possible in all cases, and consequently some teams were smaller.) Each administrator was also asked to try to pick "innovative" and hardworking teachers.

Next, a set of incentives was presented in a low-key fashion at the first meeting of the teams (and in some cases before the person agreed). Among the incentives were (1) an excellent financial stipend scheduled periodically at the completion of specific tasks and (2) attribution of work performed.

The success of any project of this nature is dependent not only upon the goodwill, cooperation, and concern of the participating teachers but also upon those same inputs from the administrators. Consequently, the same incentives were offered to the participating administrator on each team.

The basic motivational system for each team, then, consisted of three factors:

1. Small group work that was task oriented, based on empirical data that suggests that teachers value supervisors more in task-oriented situations (Harris & Hargraves, 1972).
2. A $1,500 stipend for each teacher or administrator, paid on a schedule related to major tasks completed.
3. Attribution of work. Teachers/administrators were given local public relations coverage, and names are listed on documents

produced by the project where appropriate.

Section Standard/Strategy Model

This section is concerned with the following standards/strategies:

Standard	Strategy	Outcomes/Products
1. Implementation of a system to motivate teacher participants.	Provide a schedule of financial rewards, usable products, public credit, and attribution of work.	Adherence to schedules; quality products produced.
2. Implementation of a system to involve key decision makers from schools.	Select an administrator to serve on each school team. Provide a schedule of financial rewards, usable products for programs, public credits for program, and attribution of administrator's work.	Adherence to schedules; relatively smooth process.

Procedures

The ultimate evaluation criteria for this approach, of course, would be (1) the adoption of the products by other schools and (2) the demonstration of effectiveness of the materials in meeting student learning outcomes.

The findings reported in the final report of the project (Gardner, Beatty & Warren, 1979) and described in Chapter 4 of this text suggest that the materials developed by this curriculum management system were indeed effective in helping mildly learning handicapped and disadvantaged students achieve mastery. It is, as of this writing, too early to tell whether or not the materials will be adopted by other school systems. The prospects are, however, favorable. At numerous conferences where the materials were shown, the interest from specialists in the field was most gratifying. Commercial versions of the materials are currently being developed and will be available soon. From this evaluative standpoint, then, one can conclude that the motivational system apparently worked. That is, quality products were produced using teams, and new, commercial versions are now under development for eventual distribution nationally.

From a more practical standpoint, however, other evaluative questions remain unanswered. Why do some of the personnel involved in such projects express more enthusiasm, work beyond the call of duty, and always have their materials in on time? Why do others, receiving the same incentives, fail to meet the deadlines, hand in unacceptable work, etc?

These, of course, are questions that managers always want answered and that have been the subject of numerous studies in industrial psychology. At first, we thought we might take measures on our participating teachers and administrators in an attempt to compare those who were enthusiastic and cooperative with those who were less so on factors such as adherence to time schedules, quality of work, etc. From a practical standpoint, however, the sample from our field testing was too small to make such comparisons. There was also the very real possibility that the evaluation process might alienate some of the teachers.

We did, however, make a clinical judgment. Compared to previous projects, the curriculum development process seems about the same. The range of interest and motivation of participants was from "highly enthusiastic" to "not so cooperative." One team in particular was outstanding in terms of their willingness to give of their time and effort, individually and as a group. What then makes the difference between highly enthusiastic teachers and those who are not so enthusiastic, between teams that are very effective and those that are not? We concluded that we need to know more about what motivates teachers to participate if we are to manage such projects more effectively. Moreover, we need to be able to identify the more "innovative" teachers and administrators so that we can better choose individuals and team members for future work. Recognizing these needs, we decided to study this area in more detail.

The results of our study of what motivates teachers to participate in curriculum development projects are reported in a technical article in *Education* (Gardner & Beatty, 1980b). Essentially what we did was to take a measure of innovativeness or change orientation on a group of teachers and a measure of preferred incentives. The preferred incentives of a group of eighty-eight high school teachers in rank order of preference are shown in Table I.

TABLE I
Preferred Incentive Scales*
Teacher Opinion Survey
(10 Incentive Scales) (N = 88)

Incentive Item	Mean	S.D.	Rank*
(a) How much project will help own students	2.49	1.98	1
(b) Conviction that curriculum needs changing	2.63	1.92	2
(c) Opportunity to have input into curriculum	3.23	1.90	3
(d) Opportunity to learn from university specialists	4.53	2.25	4
(e) Enjoy working with colleagues in small groups	5.08	2.37	5
(f) Released time	6.14	2.70	6
(g) Because asked by supervisor	6.16	2.28	7
(h) Amount of extra money for extra work	6.37	2.89	8
(i) Recognition, e.g. authorship of curriculum product(s)	7.52	2.40	9
(j) Recognition, e.g. name or picture in newspaper or newsletter	8.85	2.01	10

*1 = Most important incentive.
10 = Least important incentive.

Dividing the teachers into those who were found to be "innovative" and those who were not, we made comparisons between the innovative and noninnovative teachers on the preferred incentives (Table I) for becoming involved in curriculum development projects. Significant differences were found on three of the preferred incentive scales:

1. The innovators rated item (d) "Opportunity to learn from university specialist" significantly higher than did the least innovative teachers.
2. The innovative teachers were significantly more likely to rate item (e) "Enjoy working with colleagues in small groups" as a more important incentive than the least innovative teachers.
3. Last, the innovative group was more likely to give *lower* importance ratings to (h) "Amount of extra money for extra work."

(Gardner & Beatty, 1980, p. 364)

From Gardner & Beatty, Motivating teachers for vocational education of the handicapped, *Education, 100(4)*:362, 1980. Courtesy of Project Innovation, Chula Vista, CA.

Discussion

A number of authors (e.g. Brolin, 1976) suggest that the development of individualized instructional packages is an exceptionally effective way of helping learning handicapped and other students learn materials with which they are having difficulty in the regular classroom or shop. Moreover, if one asks any teacher, one will soon discover that many of them have no extra time to devote to curriculum development, yet they all will agree that the need is there. From the perspective of the curriculum development specialist, direct input from these same teachers is essential. Our management system therefore focused on the identification of "innovative" teachers as being the most likely to want to become involved and on the identification of incentives that positively affect their motivation to participate. What we found out in our pilot study was that innovative teachers do attribute interest and motivation to participate to a different set of incentives than noninnovative teachers. Thus, it is recommended that curriculum specialists focus at project start-up time on the *identification of innovative teachers* as volunteers or paid employees of the project. Moreover, the incentives used to participate should include emphasis on small group work and the use of university specialists as consultants and less emphasis on financial rewards. Other incentives should focus on explaining to teachers how much the resulting efforts will benefit students and how their participation is important in making needed curriculum changes.

LEARNING PRINCIPLES: AN ECLECTIC MODEL

Background

Most vocational programs, while highly structured and skill-mastery oriented, make some basic assumptions about language acquisition. That is, no special emphasis is placed on the acquisition of the basic vocabulary of that particular trade. It is assumed that the student will pick up *incidentally* the technical language of the shop as he or she learns how to manipulate various tools and follow through on various processes. While this assumption is probably a good one for most vocational students, it is not necessarily a good one for mildly learning handicapped and disadvantaged students. According to Brolin (1976), "incidental learning is a common problem" (p. 160) for students who have difficulty in learning. In fact, there is considerable evidence that learning disabled and educable mentally retarded students do not acquire incidental learning at the same rate as their normal high school peers (Gardner, Warren, & Gardner, 1977).

The phenomenon that mildly learning handicapped and disadvantaged students do not learn incidentally as well as their normal peers can be explained by Rotter's social learning theory (see Gardner & Beatty, 1980a). These students have been found to differ significantly from normal students on the personality variable locus of control, which has to do with attribution of reinforcement in relationship to personal inputs. They have more difficulty in attributing success or failure, rewards or punishments to their own environmental inputs than do their normal peers. They do not see the connection between what they do and the rewards they receive. Instead, the Scotts in our programs attribute rewards and reinforcements to luck, chance, fate, or the whims of powerful others (Rotter, 1966). Persons who do not see the connection between rewards and personal inputs are said to have an external locus of control. Mildly learning handicapped and disadvantaged students are more likely to have an external locus of control (Gardner & Beatty, 1980a). Moreover, persons with an external locus of control are less likely to learn incidentally from their surroundings. The implications for work training are obvious.

Recognizing this need, we theorized that (1) mildly learning handicapped and disadvantaged vocational students would require additional instruction in technical vocabulary (or technical mathematics) beyond the standard incidental approach and (2) instructional design should incorporate principles designed to give direct reinforcement for success (show the student the relationship between his own inputs and rewards). In addition to taking into consideration the implications of learning theory derived from the work of J.B. Rotter (1966), our system also used well-known and empirically based learning principles in the materials design, which is discussed later on.

Standard/Strategy Model

Standard	Strategy	Outcomes/Products
Use of learning theory and research findings as the basis for materials design.	University specialists analyze curriculum content, design basic teaching strategies and materials format in consultation with curriculum teams.	Field-tested procedures and materials.

Procedures

In adherence to this standard, an effort was made to incorporate into the design of the materials the best in learning principles and recent practices available. The approach developed by Gardner & Kurtz (1977) was used as the basic model, since the materials from that project represented a recently successful model for working with a similar student population. Based on that model the illustration of technical concepts with line drawings and the use of flash cards and tapes formed the basic design for the current project.

In addition to the empirically based design criteria of using line drawings as illustrations and flash cards, the project also emphasized an eclectic learning principles model in designing the instructional packages. No attempt will be made here to discuss the extensive research literature in instructional psychology from which these principles were derived. Brolin (1976) and Gardner & Warren (1978) offer some excellent summaries of many of these learning principles as they are adapted for students with learning handicaps. These principles are delineated in Chapter 4 of this text.

Evaluation and Discussion

Evaluation procedures for this particular strategy are synonymous with an evaluation of the materials themselves. The evaluation rests on the question of whether the materials did, in fact, accomplish what they were designed to do (see Gardner, Beatty & Warren, 1979).

The majority of the students in this project reached criterion (100% mastery of the terms) in one or two trials in all five trade areas. In addition, the treatment group as a whole made significant gains in the number of words learned, while the comparison group did not, nor did a comparison student reach criterion.

The implications of this approach are obvious. The application of well-known learning principles built around an empirically based model (Gardner & Kurtz, 1979b) is an excellent way to ensure that instructional materials are well designed and effective. Thus, we recommend this approach to the development of any curriculum change management plan.

DEVELOPING ENTRY-LEVEL VOCABULARY IN FIVE TRADE AREAS

Background

Our management plan included procedures for soliciting from the vocational teachers words that were deemed essential to entry-level employment success in each specific trade. These lists of words were then discussed with the cooperating support personnel to determine which words presented problems or might be expected to present problems to mildly learning handicapped and disadvantaged students.

The selection of a trade area for curriculum development was based on the following:

1. One of the criteria for selecting a trade area was that it should have a good job placement record.
2. Second, the vocational area should be one in which mildly learning handicapped and disadvantaged students had previously experienced difficulty.

In the early planning stages, the initial list of standards/strategies for the paradigm included "selection of content" as a strategy to be addressed. It seemed feasible and appropriate at the time to develop techniques to validate usage levels of the terminology selected as well as whether the term was "entry-level." This procedure should be equally effective in determining which mathematics skills/concepts should be chosen for curriculum modification. Eventually, time and money constraints dictated against completion of this phase of our management plan.

Standards/Strategy Model

Standard	Strategy	Outcome/Products
Selection of content to meet greatest need of students and job market.	Identification of job prospects for students related to trade area selected for development. Teacher identification of student problem area.	List of terms related to trade areas with good or high employment potential. Job descriptions for teachers. Students with problems served.
Content related to entry-level jobs and frequency of usage.	Employer validation of terms for usage and as entry-level. Professional evaluation of vocabulary coverage.	Validated list of terms.

Procedures

The first standard/strategy above was developed a priori, as were the majority of those discussed in this chapter. That is, they were for the most part predetermined in the original management plan of the project. The second standard/strategy was developed post hoc. In other words, we thought, after we had already chosen the words and begun development of the materials, that it would be a good idea to go beyond just the professional opinion of our own teams and try to establish additional data on the usage of the terms and whether or not these terms were considered entry-level by employers. Unfortunately, budget and time restrictions did not permit us to go beyond the initial piloting of the procedures used to test the entry-levelness and usage levels of the terms.

The basic procedures used to implement the above standards/strategies were as follows:

1. Teacher selection and teacher inputs into topics and word lists were made on the criteria that the topic area was one that should lead to jobs for the students and one in which students had previously experienced difficulty.
2. Professional ratings were made of the materials, including a rating on the extent of vocabulary coverage.
3. A survey instrument was developed to determine terminology usage levels.

4. A survey instrument was developed to determine whether or not employers felt that each term was necessary for entry-level job success.

Evaluation and Discussion

INITIAL VALIDATION OF TOPIC AREAS AND CONTENT. Using the procedures established by Gardner & Kurtz (1977), teachers and programs were selected on the basis of job prospects as well as other criteria discussed earlier. Thus, the initial selection of the trade areas lends support to the concept of meeting the standard of good job prospects.

In addition, the subtopical areas were defined on the basis of perceived need for supporting mildly learning handicapped and disadvantaged students in the trade areas selected. Thus this standard was validated by virtue of the initial management design.

PROFESSIONAL RATINGS – CONTENT COVERAGE. The intent of this procedure was to have materials rated by professionals in the field and to have them compare the materials to other course materials they have seen or used. Special education teachers, vocational teachers, administrators, and other interested professionals were asked to rate the vocabulary coverage, the use of tapes, flash cards, clarity of the materials, etc., on a scale developed for this purpose.

In terms of content coverage, the overwhelming majority of teachers rated the materials *better than* all other materials they had seen or used. In other words, the content coverage was considered to be superior by other professionals in the field. These ratings were obtained from participants in various workshops, conventions, and professional meetings from Maine to Florida. Thus, from the point of view of professional educators, the materials appear to be significantly on target for entry-level vocational training. This procedure would, of course, have direct application to developing self-instructional curriculum materials in technical mathematics.

VALIDATION OF TERMINOLOGY USAGE AND ENTRY-LEVEL CATEGORIZATION. Two survey instruments were developed. The first instrument was designed to be sent to employers and other experts to establish the usage level of the content. The second instrument was designed to establish whether or not the content was necessary for entry-level workers to know. Both surveys were not completed.

There were a number of factors that prevented the completion of this phase of the project. Both budget limitations and the corollary staff limitations contributed to the inability of the project staff to complete this portion of the testing of the standards/strategies model. The idea for this attempt to validate the terms in this manner (as a cross validation of the procedures used above) occurred after budgeting and after the project was well underway. Consequently, we were not equipped with a large enough budget or staff.

In spite of our own management problems, budget problems, etc., we feel that this approach is a most valuable one and that had we been able to accomplish this portion of the field testing of our model, the validation of the content would have been considerably strengthened.

In closing, we offer some suggestions for improving the survey design model that we initiated:

1. The instruments can probably be combined.
2. The list of words could be randomly assigned into smaller lists, which could then be randomly assigned to subsamples (matrix sampling). This would cut down on the work for each rater and would probably increase return rates.
3. An adequate telephone/staff/printing budget would have to be in place.

According to Dewey (1979), the following items are important considerations in designing a survey:

1. "the shorter the questionnaire, the higher the return rate."
2. "endorsements signed by prominent individuals . . . may increase return rate."
3. "simplify the wording of the questions."
4. Conduct a "pilot study to determine test-retest reliability . . . and to gain feedback on possible ambiguities of items."
5. Improve on the questionnaire format. Dewey (1979) recommends the contingency format of questionnaire design that can "facilitate the respondents' tasks in answering the questionnaire and can also improve the quality of the data produced."
6. Appearance. As Dewey points out, "Ideally, a professionally printed questionnaire is most effective in increasing response rate."
7. Color: "Yellow paper . . . had the highest percentage of returns."

These and other suggestions, succinctly summarized by Dewey (1979), should be incorporated into the development of an effective survey, which will yield useful data for curriculum content validation. The reader who is interested in pursuing this approach will find Dewey's discussion most helpful. Gardner (1981) provides an excellent model for designing a mail-telephone survey to businesses.

UNIVERSITY SUPPORT SYSTEM: INTERDISCIPLINARY TEAMS AS A FRAMEWORK FOR CHANGE

Background

Our curriculum management model, with its emphasis on product development, probably can be best described as an eclectic management model. The major goal of the model's plan was the development of quality curriculum materials that would help support the need to change an educational system to provide appropriate instruction for students with mild learning problems.

If one views the development of the materials as a major strategy for helping to institutionalize permanent change in the way these students are educated, then it seems appropriate to compare the approach to three well-known models for the management of change. According to Bolam (1975), "most changes in education take place in an organizational context" (p. 275). The typology offered by Bennis, Benne & Chin (1969) is used by Bolam to categorize major change agent strategies. He points out that while these typologies "are helpful for purposes of analysis" (p. 277), they usually do not exist in a pure form and are probably arbitrary.

One important characteristic of change agents that might be attended to is the type of authority relationship (Bolam, 1975). It may be founded on professional colleagueship, external consultancy, or administrative status. Our curriculum development model can be viewed as containing elements of all three of these authority relationships. They are best illustrated as a combination of the three typologies suggested by Bennis, Benne & Chin (1969). These typologies are paraphrased in Figure 25 and compared to the actual approaches of the management model.

Within this framework for change, our management model involved the use of interdisciplinary teams composed of university spe-

CHANGE TYPOLOGY*	ILLUSTRATIVE MANAGEMENT MODEL
EMPIRICAL RATIONAL STRATEGIES Assumes men are reasonable and will respond best to rational explanation and demonstration.	Emphasis on seeking participants who want to get involved and help improve training programs. Focus on explanation of approach and feedback on progress, etc.
NORMATIVE RE-EDUCATIVE STRATEGIES Assumes that effective change involves a change of attitudes, values, skills, etc. Typically involves a consultant-change agent who works in cooperation with schools.	University staff serve as consultants to schools and teams. Dissemination focuses on re-education of teachers/administrators not involved in materials development.
POWER-COERCIVE STRATEGIES Depends upon access to legal or administrative power.	While there are certain elements in our approach that involved these strategies (e.g. federal incentives, use of administrators on teams), the emphasis is on the above two strategies.

*See Bennis, Benne & Chin (1969).

Figure 25. Eclectic change model.

cialists (consultants), school administrators (authority personnel), and teachers (identified as innovative). All were concerned with meeting the vocational education needs of students with mild learning problems. These teams were supported by a university-based support system.

Standard/Strategies Model

Standard	Strategy	Outcomes/Products
Interdisciplinary curriculum development apoach. Both resource room and vocational education instructors provide input into curricular planning.	Small, in-school team approach.	Instructional materials for use in vocational support system in resource room or special sessions in regular teachers). Increased interdisciplinary cooperation.
University management and coordination of interdisciplinary teams	Activities coordinated by university staff, i.e. planning, eval-	Product evaluation. Curriculum products dissemination.

in the curriculum development process.	uation, design and implementation, data analysis, final product writing, etc. Verified at school level.

Procedures

According to Likert (1969), "the greatest use of human capacity consists of highly effective work groups linked together in an overlapping pattern by other similarly effective groups" (p. 356).

Likert's point succinctly describes the practical approach to curriculum development used in our model. That is, we established a series of small teams or groups dedicated to the same goals, producing quality curriculum products for use in vocational schools. The model linked them together through a university support system coupled with in-school supervisory support and cooperation. This approach was based on practical experience gained in previous projects (e.g. Gardner & Kurtz, 1977) and on the evidence that teachers are more likely to value working with supervisors and consultants in task-oriented situations (Tanner & Tanner, 1975, p. 631).

Evaluation and Discussion

It was obvious from our findings in the field testing of the model that teachers who are innovative and interested in effecting changes in the curriculum for the benefit of their students prefer to work in small groups or teams. Moreover, since teachers and school administrators rarely feel that they have the time or expertise to become involved in curriculum development changes of the nature of this project, the university/school team approach was a viable alternative to other approaches. Moreover, the advantages of an interschool/university project are obvious. The scope of the project can be broader and the potential for adaptation of the resulting products to meet the needs of the larger student population greater. In sum, on a rational-empirical basis, the interdisciplinary team/ university model seems to be a viable one for developing materials that enhance the vocational educational success of mildly learning handicapped and disadvantaged students in occupational programs. Moreover, the empirical-rational approach "has perhaps been the major approach to curriculum development in this country" (Hoyle, 1977, p. 534).

To summarize our clinical interpretation of how the small, in-school, product-oriented team approach works best, we refer the reader to some of the principles of participation cited by Doll (1978, pp. 325-326):

- Teacher participation should be used in every phase of the project.
- Teachers must work cooperatively within a climate of permissiveness, equality, and realization of personal worth.
- Teachers should be granted time, money, and facilities.
- Teachers should involve themselves in limited programs.
- Teachers should attend to specific goals and to useful materials, content, and methods.
- Teachers should use a variety of consultant and resource personnel.
- Teachers should have a coordinating body to centralize their work.

REFERENCES

Beatty, G.J., Gardner, D.C. & Avallon, J.L. National survey of the training needs of secondary regular class teachers for working with handicapped students. *College Student Journal, 15(3),* Fall, 1981.

Bennis, W., Benne, K. & Chin, R. *The Planning of Change.* New York: Holt, Rinehart and Winston, 1969.

Bolam, R. The management of educational change: Towards a conceptual framework. In Harris, A., Lawn, M. & Prescott, W. (Eds): *Curriculum Innovation.* London: Croom Helm in association with The Open University Press, 1975.

Borgen, J.A. & Davis, D.E. An investigation of curriculum development and evaluation models with implications towards a systems approach to curriculum development and evaluation of occupational education. Phase II Report. Joliet College, Illinois, ERIC ED 060201, May, 1971.

Brenton, M. Mainstreaming the handicapped. In Hass, G.: *Curriculum Planning: A New Approach* 2nd ed., Boston, MA: Allyn, 1977.

Brolin, D.E. *Vocational Preparation of Retarded Citizens.* Columbus, OH: Merrill, 1976.

Dewey, B.E. Factors affecting initial employment in special education. Unpublished doctoral dissertation, Boston University, 1979.

Doll, R. *Curriculum Improvement: Decision Making and Process.* Boston, MA: Allyn, 1978.

Fryer, F.W. *An Evaluation of Level of Aspiration as a Training Procedure.* Englewood

Cliffs, NJ: Prentice-Hall, 1964.

Gardner, D.C. & Beatty, G.J. Locus of control change techniques: Important variables in work training. *Education, 100(3):* 237-242, 1980a.

Gardner, D.C. & Beatty, G.J. Motivating teachers for vocational curriculum development for the handicapped. *Education, 100(4),* 1980b.

Gardner, D.C. & Beatty, G.J. Practical approaches to curriculum development: A management handbook. Final Report, Project HIRE, Vol. 2, USOE Grant #G007701947, Boston, MA: Boston University School of Education, June, 1979. *Resources in Education,* August, 1980, ERIC ED 183 739.

Gardner, D.C., Beatty, G.J. & Warren, S.A. Vocational curriculum modification: Teaching technical language to learning handicapped students. Final Report, Vol. 1, Project HIRE, USOE Grant No. G007701947, Boston, MA: Boston University School of Education, September, 1979. *Resources in Education,* August, 1980, ERIC ED 183 738.

Gardner, D.C. & Kurtz, M.A. An evaluation of a curriculum model for teaching phototypesetting to handicapped students. *Education, 99(3):* 314-320, 1979a.

Gardner, D.C. & Kurtz, M.A. Teaching technical vocabulary to handicapped students. *Reading Improvement,* 61-65, Fall, 1979.

Gardner, D.C. & Kurtz, M.A. Vocational curriculum models and assessment procedures handbook for handicapped students. Final Report: Project VITA: A cooperative activities model for university and vocational/technical school collaboration. Boston, MA: Boston University School of Education, July, 1977. USOE Grant No. G007500558.

Gardner, D.C. & Warren, S.A. *Careers and Disabilities: A Career Education Approach.* Stamford, CT: Greylock Pubs, 1978.

Gardner, D.C., Warren, S.A. & Gardner, P.L. Locus of control and law knowledge: A comparison of normal, retarded, and learning disabled adolescents. *Adolescence, 12(45):* 103-109, 1977.

Gardner, P.L. Employment of handicapped persons: A survey of characteristics and opinions of supervisors from small urban manufacturing firms. Unpublished doctoral dissertation, Boston University, 1981.

Hoyle, E. How does the curriculum change: Part 1: A proposal for inquired. In Bellack, A. and Kliebard, H. (Eds): *Curriculum and Education.* Berkeley, CA: McCutchan, 1977.

Likert, R. The nature of highly effective groups. In Carver, F. & Sergiovanni, T.: *Organizations and Human Behavior: Focus on Schools.* New York: McGraw-Hill, 1969.

Rotter, J.B. Generalized expectancies for internal versus external control of reinforcement. *Psychological Monographs, 80(1),* 1966.

Tanner, D. & Tanner, L. *Curriculum Development: Theory into Practice.* New York: MacMillian, 1975.

CHAPTER 6

MAINSTREAMING IN THE COMMUNITY: MYTHS VERSUS FACTS ON HIRING HANDICAPPED AND DISADVANTAGED YOUTH

OVERVIEW

IN 1973, Congress enacted the Rehabilitation Act (P.L. 93-112), which extended to handicapped individuals the same protections afforded racial groups and other minorities by the Civil Rights Act of 1964. Section 504 of the act mandates nondiscriminatory employment practices regarding handicapped workers:

> No otherwise qualified handicapped individual in the United States . . . shall solely by reason of his handicap, be excluded from participation in, be denied the benefits of, or be subjected to discrimination under any program or activity receiving Federal financial assistance. (Sec. 84.4(a))

At the same time, predictions about the employability of the 2.5 million handicapped students entering the world of work in the five years following the passage of the act were indeed bleak (Barone, 1973):

1. Employed or in college 21%
2. Underemployed at the poverty level 40%
3. Idle or at home 8%
4. Unemployed and on welfare 26%
5. Totally dependent and institutionalized 5%

At this writing, we have no current comparable employment forecasts for the 1980s. However, it is our professional opinion that there has been and will be little change in the employment status of handicapped students leaving our schools in light of today's inflationary economy. What these employment projections suggest is that despite our current professional efforts and legislation, about 79 percent of the handicapped students leaving our system in the 1980s may in fact be unemployed or underemployed. Couple these statistics with those of the many disadvantaged youth on welfare, and the scope of the problem becomes overwhelming.

This problem is not new. Nearly forty years ago, Richard

Hungerford was concerned with providing appropriate vocational training for handicapped youth. Among his many concerns were vocational placement and career guidance to prepare these youth for "survival in an occupationally oriented society" (Gardner, 1977). In the interim period between Hungerford's pioneering efforts and the present, we have attempted to use federal and state monies to design, develop, refine, and improve educational programs and services that would ultimately make their mark on the employment status of handicapped and disadvantaged youth. Yet when you examine the *bottom line,* not much has changed.

Disadvantaged and handicapped youth by the thousands are underemployed or unemployed. Many are desperate for the opportunity to enter the mainstream of our work-oriented culture but do not have the requisite training or understanding of the work world to adjust successfully. Our system of job placement for normal adults is nothing short of madness. (Have you looked for a job for yourself lately?) For the handicapped or disadvantaged youth without saleable skills and appropriate job-seeking skills, the problem remains almost insurmountable.

The obvious question, then, is, What can we do? Is it possible to change these gruesome employment statistics for handicapped and disadvantaged youth in the coming decade? We think it is, but it will take more than federal and state monies pumped into CETA and other stopgap programs. The percentage of disadvantaged and handicapped youth receiving vocational training must be increased. More important, however, we must attend to the real world of work, that is, follow Hungerford's model and deal directly with employers (Gardner, 1977).

EMPLOYERS ARE PEOPLE TOO: THERE ARE TWO SIDES TO EVERY STORY

A good salesperson to a certain extent has divided loyalties. He or she must be loyal to the company and its products or it becomes impossible to generate enough enthusiasm to convince the potential buyer that the product or service is worth the investment. Simultaneously, the salesperson must look for, ascertain, understand, and meet the needs of the customer or there will be no sale. In many instances the needs of the company may conflict with the needs of the buyer. The same situation exists when professionals try to place a student or recent graduate in a job, yet many professionals see only the client's side of the story. Thus in our college classes comments come from both experienced and inexperienced human service professionals who almost always infer that the reason handicapped or disadvantaged youth are unemployed has nothing to do with "us" (the teacher/rehab. counselor, etc.) but has to do with "them," the "uncaring businesspeople." This kind of stereotyping of businesspeople is more common than we would like to admit. Somewhere in our efforts to be do-gooders we forget that America is the land of opportunity, a free enterprise economy, and that what makes America great is the profit incentive. It creates real jobs, provides the tax dollars for our social programs, and creates the incentives for the many talented Americans who invent and produce the material goods that most of us want. We live in the freest and most affluent society in the history of mankind, yet we hypothesize that a large percentage of those in human services think of the terms *business, profits,* and *free enterprise* as dirty words. This kind of attitude on the part of professionals, coupled with employers' fears and stereotypical reactions to handicapped and disadvantaged workers, leads to the following kind of dialogue:

Business Person: "Sure, I care about the less fortunate but I have a business to run."

Human Service Worker: "That's all they ever think about . . . profits."

Business Person: "I don't know how to handle them and I don't know how reliable they are."

Human Service Worker: "He doesn't really care about people."

Business Person: "We had one who worked here once and he had a lot of psychological problems and we had to let him go."

Human Service Worker: "See that, one bad experience and he won't risk his money on my client."

Business Person: "This is a small operation and everyone has to do his part without a lot of supervision. I just don't know if a handicapped person could handle it here."

Human Service Worker: "All he cares about is production. I know my client can do it . . . why can't he see it?"

As one can deduce from the hypothetical dialogue above, the problem is twofold:

The Human Service Perspective

For most teachers, counselors, and other human service personnel, the issue tends to be clouded by the stereotypical perspective that employers' attitudes need to be changed. Thus, employers become the object of the verb *change* when translated into actual practice. The "break down negative attitudes" syndrome abounds in the literature (e.g. see Gardner, 1981). No doubt this approach has some substance. Some employers are reluctant to hire handicapped and disadvantaged workers. Some employers are, in fact, quite negative about the concept. Many, however, are not. We, as placement specialists, need to adopt the attitude that employers are people, too. They are our parents, siblings, children, and friends, and the great majority of them will help their fellowman if they have the opportunity. Frequently they need our help to do that. In fact, it is our job to make it as easy as possible for them to help our students.

The Employer's Perspective

From the employer's perspective, teachers and counselors are often viewed as unrealistic do-gooders who have negative opinions about businesses. Businesspeople simply do not trust the human service culture. They believe that teachers, for example, do not know about or understand our economic system or the importance of profits. Businesspeople are also under the impression that teachers don't *like* the profit system (Cushing, 1980). Businesses are in business to make a profit. In a free enterprise system, the *raison d'etre* of business is profits. Not only are profits legal, they are essential to our economic growth. When profits disappear, our human service programs disappear. Jobs disappear. For some reason human service personnel are not able to understand or relate to this concept. Until they do, the job of helping handicapped and disadvantaged persons make the transition from school to productive employment remains at best an extremely frustrating experience for many employers, teachers, counselors, and students. This next section offers some comments and tips on how to minimize some of the frustration of the process.

MATCHING JOBS AND PEOPLE

In a recent study of 100 manufacturing firms in the Greater Boston area (Gardner, 1981), employers expressed very positive attitudes over the telephone about hiring and working with handicapped persons. When asked to respond to a detailed questionnaire about the topic, however, their attitudes were considerably more resistant (conservative) than those of supervisors in a nonprofit organization. This recent study is illustrative of the many studies completed over the past decade. Employers simply have to be sold on matching a handicapped or disadvantaged worker to their company in specific jobs. A successful match is usually the result of a lot of hard work on the part of the student, the potential employer, and the placement specialist.

Quality Matchmaking

If a handicapped/disadvantaged student is going to be successful in entering the world of work, he or she *must be effective* on the job. Being effective is directly dependent on the quality of the match between the employee and the job. Handicapped and disadvantaged students, like other workers, bring their own set of needs, skills, and experiences to the job. The match will be most successful to the degree that the student's needs and personal goals mesh with the needs and goals of the organization and the job.

The problem of achieving a quality match is incredibly complex. The problem has not been addressed in a scientific way by our society. We can send an astronaut to the moon easier than we can expedite the job-matching process. We cling to the same old one-page resume process that our fathers used. Thus, job hunting remains an art form of the past while space exploration has already entered the twenty-first century.

Who Matches Whom?

Fortunately for the handicapped/disadvantaged vocational student, the system of job matching/placement usually includes a middleman or, shall we say, a matchmaker. This professional matchmaker may be a teacher or counselor or other specialist. The most common title is coordinator. Whatever the title, this person functions as a matchmaker between the employer and the potential employee, the vocational student. Thus the responsibility for matchmaking is threefold:

Student Responsibilities	Employer Responsibilities	Coordinator Responsibilities
Choose wisely. Self-honesty. Actively participate in goal assessment. Help employer make necessary changes where applicable in job.	Choose wisely. Set clear-cut goals and communicate them to employee. Listen to and encourage employee to grow. Offer suggestions for job redesign where applicable. Flexibility.	Choose match wisely. Listen to student and listen to employer carefully. Help each establish clear-cut goals before, during, and after match. Offer suggestions for job redesign where applicable. Provide training and follow-up.

Matching Jobs to People or People to Jobs?

This question will undoubtedly always be asked. The answer is both. Yes, people can be matched to jobs. Yes, jobs can be matched to people. The process usually involves both. From the employer's perspective, often the easiest way, on the surface, is to look for the right person for the job. Unfortunately, there is no standard way of dealing with this process. Work situations vary and change rapidly, particularly in our culture. There is the culture of the organization itself, the culture of region, and the individual and varying needs and values of the people who make up the particular work force or group.

There is always the constant pressure of change in our highly technological society. Jobs become radically different or disappear almost overnight. People change and grow over time, sometimes as rapidly as our technology. All people resist change; the role of the manager, thus, has *become not how to manage but how to manage change.*

Within this context, there are some options, however. The student-employee, the employer, and the coordinator can address the issue of matching *goals,* at least short-term ones. The student can list a number of goals toward which he is working. These can be matched to the employer's immediate needs or goals. These can be tied to tasks required by the employer and matched to student skills (or skills to be learned and then performed by the student-employee). The job of the coordinator then becomes one of matching goals and developing or suggesting strategies for meeting the shared goals. This may involve providing additional training for the vocational student and/or helping the student and the employer redesign a job or a family of jobs. The procedures for job redesign go something like this:

1. The coordinator works with the student to assess his or her work potential. He/she helps the student list vocational skills and limitations and occupational goals.
2. Working with the employer, the coordinator helps the employer analyze relevant jobs and list the tasks required to perform those jobs.
3. Working with the employer and the student, the coordinator helps them identify the tasks in each job that the student can perform or learn to perform rapidly.
4. Last, the family of jobs is redesigned so that *one* of the new jobs is composed of tasks that the hanidcapped or disadvantaged student can perform (see Fig. 26).

Matchmaker: Develop a Sales Pitch

We know that this concept is difficult for many professionals in schools and other human services agencies to accept, but the bottom line (to use business terminology) is that the coordinator or placement specialist needs to be a sales-oriented person. By this we mean you must be able to listen well so that you can sell well. You must recognize that your role in placing a student is very similar to the role of a sales representative for an industrial firm. You are, in fact, a middleman/woman. You are trying to find a match between the needs of your student for a satisfying job and the needs of the potential employer for an employee who will be satisfactory.

Learn How to Sell

Provided you have determined that the job is right for your client/student, your task is to sell the match to the potential em-

I. IDENTIFY JOB TASKS WHICH CAN BE PERFORMED BY THE HANDICAPPED/DISADVANTAGED STUDENT*

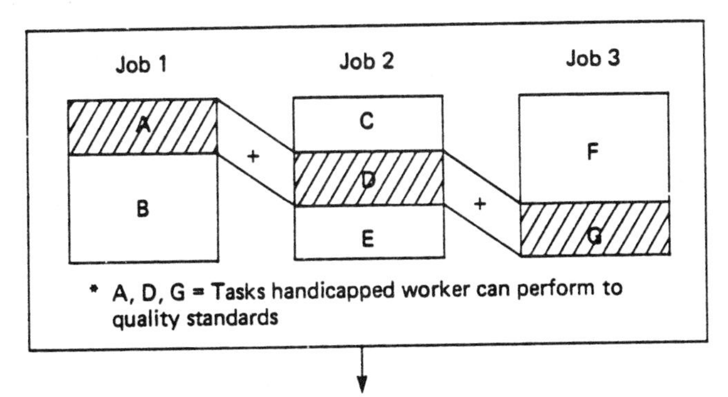

II. REDESIGN JOBS AND ASSIGN HANDICAPPED/DISADVANTAGED WORKER TO A NEW JOB

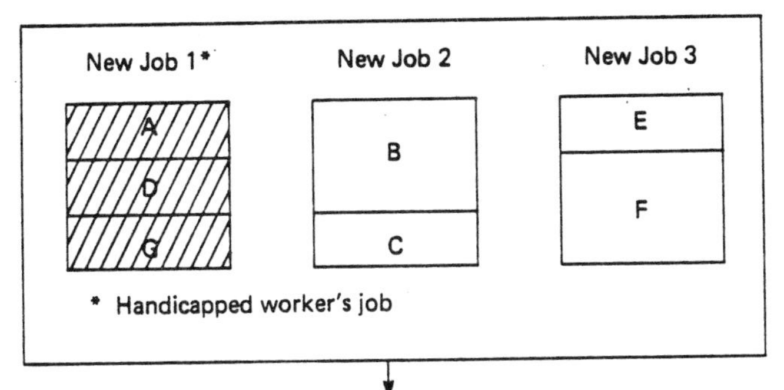

III. PROVIDE TRAINING FOR HUMAN RESOURCE PERSONNEL ON TECHNIQUES DEVELOPED SO THAT COMPANY CAN REDESIGN ON ITS OWN WITH FUTURE EMPLOYEES

Figure 26. Job redesign model for handicapped/disadvantaged workers.

ployer. Below are some tips on selling:

1. Find out what the employer *really* needs in the way of an employee. Go over in your mind the skills and needs of your clients (students) and see if they match the employer's needs. *Don't* sell him on a student who doesn't match!
2. Do not make long nonstop sales pitches. Practice developing a sales approach process that creates dialogue. Your goal is to elicit a series of questions from the employer that will reveal his true needs and attitudes. You need to acquire hard data on his

requirements so that you can seek a match between your client's needs and skills and the employer's requirements.

3. Try to identify all the hiring influences in the organization. You need to know who will *really* make the decision. If more than one person is involved, you need to talk to them all.
4. You will need to know who will be *directly* supervising your student/client. And you must have an opportunity to talk with the supervisor before making a decision to place your student. Many placements at first appear ideal from the perspective of the company's personnel department and the school representative. When the student is placed under a specific supervisor, however, everything seems to go wrong. By all means make it your policy to study the supervisor carefully before making a match.
5. Never make a match when the person doing the hiring (or the person who will be supervising your student) makes a lot of negative objections but hires your student anyway. Handicapped and disadvantaged students should never be placed where they are being hired to fill some quota or out of charity or sympathy. Your client should be sold to the employer because you believe that your client/student will make a darned good employee for that organization.
6. Learn to stay alert to verbal and body language signals that indicate that the employer is ready to hire. The placement specialist who continues selling beyond that point may in fact not be able to place his or her student. Every good salesperson knows these signals. Oversell can kill the match.
7. The main reasons that people are unable to close a deal, whether it is selling a product or a student, are that they (1) talk too much, (2) do not listen enough, (3) are unable to identify the hidden influences that will affect the decision to hire, and (4) fail to pay attention to the signals that indicate that the employer is ready to do business.

Selling Your Program

Many of the first jobs held by handicapped and disadvantaged youth are the result of a part-time placement by the school or other agency. These part-time jobs are supervised by a school or agency professional (the coordinator), and in many cases academic credit is given. The most common are cooperative education programs and work study programs. While definitions vary across the country, cooperative education usually means academic credit for paid work in an area directly related to the curriculum, while work study means academic credit for paid work that may not be directly related to the student's curriculum. If your rôle is to place handicapped or disadvantaged students in cooperative or work study jobs, then part of your sales pitch will be to sell the school's program as well as the individual student. You will need to develop a sales pitch to explain to business and other potential employers the advantages of collaboration with the school or agency you represent. Below are some of the obvious advantages to the major beneficiaries of your program – businesses, the school, and the students.

For the school, the advantages of cooperative or work study programs include (1) good public relations opportunities, (2) a way to offer direct services to the community, (3) a cost-effective way to train students, (4) an opportunity to gain feedback from the business world on the curriculum's effectiveness and to keep up with our rapidly changing technology, and (5) a method to keep many students from dropping out of school.

For the student, the advantages are both short-term and long-term. Students get an opportunity to (1) earn money and learn to accept responsibility, (2) acquire appropriate work attitudes and work habits, (3) gain knowledge of the world of work and explore careers, and (4) learn how to get along with peers and supervisors on the job.

For businesses and other employers, the advantages of collaboration with the school or other training agencies include the opportunity to (1) obtain better full-time workers from a pool of part-time workers without making a permanent contract with any one single student beyond the cooperative education assignment, (2) have access to the school's or agency's support system, including counseling and training, (3) refine and validate the company's own training methods in consultation with the school's professional representative, (4) improve the community image of the company through participation in the school's program (P.R.), and (5) comply with applicable state and federal regulations (e.g. Section 504 of the Rehabilitation Act of 1973).

CASE STUDIES

The following case studies illustrate some of the common problems you will face in helping handicapped and disadvantaged students enter the world of work. These case studies are fictionalized compilations of actual cases that took place just a few years ago – before the legal mandate to mainstream. Consequently, you will find that the students mentioned in the case studies were often put into special classes. You can use these case studies as a way to springboard discussions and to reflect on the complex problem of placement. The questions at the end of each case study are designed to assist you in developing an awareness of the many ways in which you can approach a placement problem. Some points to be noted in the studies follow:

Employers are concerned with the basics first:

- Will he/she steal from me?
- Can he/she accept responsibility . . . come to work on time?
- How long will it take to train her/him?
- Can he/she get along with customers?
- Can he/she get along with fellow workers?

Some employers will not change their negative attitudes about handicapped and disadvantaged workers.

- Employers with negative attitudes may transfer these opinions across a wide range of behaviors (the handicapped or disadvantaged worker is condemned to failure in advance).
- Some people are just not nice. They treat all employees the same – badly!

Employers' attitudes can be changed in some cases.

- Excellent productivity on the part of one handicapped or disadvantaged worker can serve to break down the stereotype for others.
- Placement personnel can help by trying to match carefully the handicapped/disadvantaged worker/job/employer.

Placement personnel and the handicapped/disadvantaged workers must be prepared for failure and retrial.

- No job is perfect.
- No boss is perfect.
- No employee is perfect.

- Some people are great at one job and awful at another.

Case 1 — Jimmy

Personal History/Family Background

When Jimmy entered the work study program, he was sixteen years old. He was withdrawn, hardly speaking to anyone. He did not cause any problems in class. In fact, he was so quiet that the high school resource room instructor thought at first that he had a hearing problem and thus had little if any speech. He was an attractive 5 foot 9 inch young man, lithe (about 135 pounds), and not very athletic. He had sandy brown straight hair, brown eyes, and good health. Jimmy entered the work study program at the high school in the second year of its inception. He was categorized under the label of "disadvantaged/culturally deprived" and was placed in a program where he attended morning classes until 11:00 am and then worked outside of the school for the remainder of the day.

Jimmy was born to Rebecca and Fred during a period of crisis in their marriage. At the age of two Jimmy went to live with his grandmother (Rebecca's mother). His mother had removed him from the house because she felt that he was in physical danger from his father. Shortly thereafter she left Fred. Because of Fred's history of wife beating, divorce followed shortly. Rebecca went to work, leaving Jimmy with two older women, his grandmother and her nurse.

When Jimmy was four years old, Rebecca married Barry, a longshoreman. The family moved again. Because of his alcoholism, Barry lost his job. Two years later Rebecca and Barry were divorced. Rebecca went to work again, leaving Jimmy with his elderly aunt and her nurse. He was enrolled in kindergarten at age six and found to be quite inhibited and shy. Jimmy passed first and second grade with much effort. At the end of the second grade, his mother married for the third time to Robert. This marriage ended within eighteen months due to Rebecca's fear that her new husband, Robert, would hurt Jimmy because he resented him so much. Rebecca then went to work as a housekeeper for an older disabled couple who resided in a poor section of a small suburban town. For the duration of his upper elementary and junior/senior high school years, Jimmy and his mother shared a first-floor one-bedroom apartment with a kitchenette. The older couple lived upstairs. Rebecca and Jimmy lived rent free in this old, shabby, unkempt house in return for housekeeping and nursing services Rebecca provided the couple. In addition to her free room and board, she received $25 a week.

Rebecca could barely read and write. She did not have a checking account, and she kept her money hidden in the house. Jimmy's clothes were old and worn, and at Christmastime they received help from a local charity.

School History

School records are scattered and not very informative for Jimmy's first five years in school. Jimmy was not a problem student. He seemed to get along with peers and teachers. Most of his early school records point to a boy who was inhibited, shy, inactive, and slow to develop speech. In the fourth grade, Jimmy's standardized tests show that he was performing slightly below grade level in reading, spelling, and English.

As a junior high student, Jimmy remained quiet, passive, and uninterested in school activities. He received special tutoring in reading, spelling, and language arts. He was given speech therapy, which he disliked intensely.

In high school, Jimmy's image began to change. He grew into an attractive, tall, lanky teenager. He began to hang around with boys in some of his classes who were considered by most teachers as "the losers." He was, however, still basically reserved and was more often found to be following the rest of the pack and not really expressing himself freely.

Jimmy was accepted by this group of tough teenagers. He tried to please them and to go along with what they said and did, both inside and outside of school. The behavior patterns became ominous, and his advisor began to push Jimmy towards joining the work study program. He would then be exposed to working adults and be able to make new friends who might provide better role models.

Work Experience/Job Placement

Due to Jimmy's previous history, his mama's boy syndrome, and poor relationships or lack of relationships with male authority figures, it was decided that a perfect placement for him would be in a male-oriented work environment. The teacher/coordinator of the work study program for disadvantaged students chose a service station job for him.

Placing a disadvantaged student in a work situation illustrates some of the many ways in which disadvantaged youth are stereotyped. First, the owner of the gas station was concerned that Jimmy could be trusted. He had had previous negative experiences with high school workers who had stolen from him. The owner felt that Jimmy was a perfect candidate to become a thief, since he was economically deprived.

This proved not to be a problem. Eventually, Jimmy was the one who closed the station at night and was trusted with adding the daily receipts and putting them in the safe along with all of the cash. The owner of the station was so pleased by Jimmy's performance that he gave him a set of keys to the station. Jimmy's trustworthiness set the foundation for a long and positive relationship between the station owner and Jimmy. After Jimmy worked there for about six months, he discovered that the owner himself had been brought up in a culturally disadvantaged home environment and had made it on his own. The station owner admitted that he saw a lot of himself in Jimmy.

Jimmy's spoken English was poor. He constantly used words such as *nuttin* for *nothing, ain't* for *isn't, none* for *any, them* for *those,* etc. The owner of the station wanted Jimmy to speak pleasantly to all customers and was especially concerned with the image presented by the use of poor grammar. He spent many years trying to perfect his own grammar, and he expected all of his employees to work on theirs. He felt that his customers would be alienated by a teenager who, as the owner so bluntly stated, "sounds dumb." It was suggested that Jimmy's resource room teacher work with him on becoming more proficient in his spoken language. As it turned out, Jimmy made marked improvement just because he "wanted to sound smart," not "dumb," and because he really enjoyed the job, the learning of new skills, and the friends he had made.

After Jimmy graduated from high school, he continued to be the night service station attendant. During the gasoline shortage when many workers were being laid off, the station owner sent Jimmy to evening school for bookkeeping and clerical record keeping. Eventually, Jimmy did the books each day. In addition, he took the cash receipts to the bank when the owner was away or not available. The owner of the station tried Jimmy on several different jobs at the station and found that he was best suited doing the bookkeeping at night and servicing the cars at the gas pump.

CASE STUDY QUESTIONS: Jimmy

1. What other occupations do you think would be suitable for Jimmy?

   Name at least 4 occupations.

   1. ______________ 3. ______________

   2. ______________ 4. ______________

2. Explain and discuss your rationale for selecting each occupation.

   1. ______________________________

   ____

   2. ______________________________

   ____

   3. ______________________________

   ____

   4. ______________________________

3. What would be the ideal educational program for Jimmy assuming he has been placed in a work study program leading to one of the above occupations?

____

____

____

____

____

____

____

____

4. What kind of ancillary services would you consider important to Jimmy's maximum career development?

____

____

____

____

____

5. What do you consider to be the "key" element in making a successful match between Jimmy's needs and a potential employer?

____

____

6. Would you have made the same placement for Jimmy as the one in this case study? ____ Yes ____ No

Explain. ______________________________________

____

____

____

Case 2 — Douglas

Personal History/Family Background

When Douglas entered the work study program, he was seventeen years old, outgoing, and very likable. He had been placed in a special class in his second year of elementary school because he was falling far behind and had remained in a special class since that time. This was his first experience in an integrated/special needs mainstreaming program in a public high school. Doug was tall (6 feet, 2 inches), thin (about 160 pounds), and very uncoordinated. He was a nice-looking and very neat young man who was always meticulous about having his shirt tucked into his pants and having no creases in either his shirt or his pants. His hair was always stylishly in place and his hands and nails clean. He was in excellent health. He was asked to enter the work study program when he was in the third year of high school. His advisor felt that he was ready to face the outside working world.

Doug was born to Mary and Jeremy in the first year of their teenage marriage. Looking back on his birth, Mary and Jeremy felt that he wouldn't have been retarded if they had waited a few years. Doug was a year old when his brother Philip was born. A year later his sister Jamie arrived. Eighteen months after Jamie came another girl, Theresa, and the fifth child, a boy named Ronnie, was born when Doug was nine. Doug's mother had four children under the age of five, and her memories are of years of drudgery: cooking, washing, cleaning, and sheer exhaustion. During these years, she did notice a difference in the developmental rate between Doug, Philip, and Jamie. Jamie and Philip were doing things at earlier ages than Doug, such as talking, sitting, walking, eating with utensils, etc. When she told her pediatrician he said that "all children develop at different rates, don't worry, Doug will eventually catch up." Doug never did catch up to his brothers and sisters. By the time he was in the second grade the teacher suggested he be placed in a special class because he was failing second grade and could not keep up with the other children.

Mary and Jeremy were very devoted and close to all of their children. Doug was never left out of anything. The parents were most supportive. They truly loved him and did for him what they did for all their children. The family was very religious and went to church regularly. Mary felt that she was chosen by God to have this mentally retarded child because she had enough love and understanding in her heart to give the child a warm and loving home. This attitude is interesting and of course important. He did not grow up believing he was a burden to the family, but rather he felt as if he were another contributing member who just happened to be slower than the others. All of his brothers and sisters adored him. He was a bit apprehensive about going to work, but he received a lot of encouragement at home from his father, who had risen to become a vice-president of a large corporation.

School History

Doug's reading and math were around the third grade level. His speech was excellent, and he was always able to verbalize his feelings and opinions.

Doug had many friends both inside and outside of the resource room. This was largely due to the popularity of Philip and Jamie, who were also in high school. Doug was also popular with the other special needs students. He was always willing to help out others if he could, and he enjoyed being with other people. The resource room teacher described Doug as a "super guy."

Work Experience/Job Placement

Doug had a preconceived notion (probably given to him at an early age) that he would be going to work at a religious seminary and eventually would study to be a priest. With Doug's outgoing and friendly personality it was felt that he would work well with the public if given a situation where he felt secure and not pressured.

During the Christmas season, Doug was placed in a department store located a half mile from his home and a half mile from the high school. His parents were anxious for him to work and were agreeable to any job that the work study coordinator felt was appropriate for his skill level. The job involved stockroom work out on the main floor. Doug was required to bring boxes from the stockroom, which were given to him by the stockroom clerk, go to a department head clerk, and ask where the boxes were to be placed in that department.

When Doug was placed on the job, he was described to the personnel manager as pleasant, responsible, friendly, and reliable. She was told that he was a vocational student who was not college bound.

She was also told that he did not function well under pressure and that he should be given one job/task to master at a time.

All of this was agreed upon, and the work coordinator brought Doug in to sign all the forms and meet the personnel manager. When the personnel manager saw Doug, she immediately became rude, formal, and nervous. After Doug finished the application forms, he went to the stockroom clerk to begin training. The personnel manager and coordinator then had a discussion. The personnel manager said that she knew Doug and his family and that she knew he was *retarded.* It was pointed out that if she knew his family, she would know what a fine family it was. All she kept saying was that she didn't want any retarded people out on the floor working during the Christmas season because it was bad for the store's image. She felt he would probably be better off in some other job and that she had nothing against "them" (mentally retarded people), but they should go where it is appropriate. When asked what that meant, she said, "Where they won't be a bother to everyone and can work at their own pace." The stockroom clerk, however, found Doug to be a refreshing change from the, as he put it, "rude and lazy kids" who usually work for him.

After much discussion, the personnel manager agreed to put Doug on a two-week trial. It was during the second week that an incident took place that resulted in Doug's being fired.

Doug was accused by the personnel manager of influencing another high school student (who was *not* in the special needs class) to expose himself in front of a customer. Even though Doug claimed to be totally unaware of the other student's actions, the personnel manager fired him immediately.

Subsequently, Doug was placed in a food service company where he was trained to prepare gelatin dessert for a school lunch program. The company manager, as a father of twelve, was understanding and knew that each person has special needs and that each person can do well in the right situation. He tried hard to help Doug adjust. He placed him in a room working with three very nice women who took Doug under their wings. They trained him and worked with him for two years, at which time he entered a cook's helper training program. Doug is presently in this training program. When he graduates he hopes to be able to find employment in a large kitchen in a restaurant, hotel, or hospital.

CASE STUDY QUESTIONS: Douglas

1. What other occupations do you think would be suitable for Doug?

   Name at least 4 occupations.

   1. ______________________ 3. ______________________

   2. ______________________ 4. ______________________

2. Explain and discuss your rationale for selecting each occupation.

   1. ____

   ____

   2. ____

   ____

   3. ____

   ____

   4. ____

   ____

3. What would be the ideal educational program for Doug, assuming he has been placed in a work study program leading to one of the above occupations?

____

____

____

____

____

____

____

____

4. What kind of ancillary services would you consider important to Doug's maximum career development?

____

____

____

5. What do you consider to be the key element in making a successful match between Doug and any potential employer?

____

____

6. Would you have placed Doug in the department store?

 _____ Yes _____ No

 Explain. ________________________________

____

____

7. How do you think Doug's firing should be discussed with him? How should you deal with the personnel manager?

____

____

Case 3 — Wendy

Personal History/Family Background

When Wendy entered the work study program, she was an aggressive, outspoken, sixteen-year-old teenager. She had been removed from school for poor behavior and attendance on numerous occasions. She was small (5 feet), and stocky (135 pounds). She had long dark hair, which she rarely combed, dark eyes, and dark skin. Her advisor hoped that if she would become part of the work study program it would provide the incentive for her to stay in school. She was classified as (economically) disadvantaged.

Wendy was born to a Caucasian mother (Maria) and a Native American named Jed. Maria and Jed had nine children within a thirteen-year period. Wendy was the first. She was followed by eight boys. After the ninth child, the mother become very ill and was hospitalized in a sanitarium for about two years. After her release, she continued to be emotionally unstable and attempted to commit suicide on several occasions. Jed worked on the docks unloading ships. The family lived in a tenement housing project in a slum neighborhood. The apartment had four rooms. Wendy slept on the floor in the living room with her two youngest brothers. The remaining five boys slept in one bedroom on mattresses on the floor. The parents had the other bedroom. The kitchen was small. They had only four chairs so the family ate in shifts or at the counter in the kitchen.

Maria drank heavily and was not able to take care of her young children's needs. Wendy was often forced to stay home from school to take care of the younger children. By eleven years of age, Wendy shopped weekly for the food, cleaned the house, washed the clothes, and cooked the food for her family. Her schoolwork suffered because she not only had to take care of the children's needs and the house but she also had to take care of her mother.

Her father stayed out late many nights and had on occasion threatened to divorce the wife if she didn't "shape up." Maria had Wendy when she was sixteen, and when Wendy was sixteen she too became pregnant. Her mother wanted to throw her out of the house, but her father prevented this. She had an abortion and remained at home. When Wendy was seventeen her mother was sent back to the sanitarium, and her father filed for divorce. Jed got custody of all the children.

Her father brought his girlfriend, Karen, home, and shortly thereafter he married her. She took over all of the chores and tasks that Wendy had previously done. Karen was a few years older than Jed. She had been married before but had no children. She worked as a secretary in a clothing manufacturing company. Jed and Karen eventually moved into a larger place, a two-family house. Although the neighborhood was old and dirty, Karen fixed up the place, and for the first time each child had a bed to sleep in.

School History

Wendy was not placed in a special class until the fifth grade when she really fell behind in all of her subjects because she was at home taking care of the house and children. When the school suggested that Wendy might be retarded, the parents agreed to have her tested. The tests showed that Wendy was a socially normal, physically normal, and academically slow, but not retarded, eleven-year-old. In reading and language arts she was a grade below her age group, and in arithmetic she was about one-half year behind. Because there was only one program for slower children, she was placed in a special class.

By sixth grade, Wendy had started hanging around with the wrong crowd and was getting into trouble in school. She found the special class work easy. She planned to quit school at the end of junior high. Because Wendy was going around with older kids, she happened to meet the teacher of the special class at the high school. The high school teacher and Wendy developed an immediate rapport. Wendy told her that one of the reasons she was quitting school was because of the junior high school special needs teacher. Wendy felt that the teacher hated her. She claimed that the teacher was always making fun of her clothes, figure, hair, etc. Wendy and the teacher had had bitter arguments in class, and she had been suspended on more than one occasion for "giving this teacher a piece of her mind."

With the support and encouragement of the high school special class teacher, Wendy did not quit school and enrolled the following year in the high school special class program. She was given the opportunity to be part of the career training program for handicapped students, which was in its second year, and was enrolled in a clerical program. For one year she took courses in typing, filing, basic record keeping, and elementary shorthand.

Wendy performed at about the fifth or sixth grade level in language arts and arithmetic. Although she had some minor trouble in some of her classes because of her outspoken behavior, she passed all of her clerical program subjects except elementary shorthand. Although she saw the school counselor at least once a week, his case load was so large that he was able to give her only cursory attention.

Because of her poor track record, Wendy was placed in the work study program on a probationary basis. She signed a contract that said she would be allowed to go to work only if her grades improved and if her behavior in school improved.

Work Experience/Job Placement

Her advisor felt that Wendy would do well in a situation where she could work alone but would be given a lot of support by a female/maternal authority figure. Unfortunately, the only job available at that time was in a small office with a male manager. Wendy's job was to answer the phone, to take messages, and to make appointments for customers. The job also included some filing and typing items such as labels for file folders. For the first few days everything seemed to be going well. She said that when the office manager came in he gave her work, left for about two hours, and then came back to check to see who called, what she did, and to close the office for the night. The reason he wanted a work study student from the high school, he said, was that the office was not always busy, and it was too expensive to have a full-time receptionist.

About the third or fourth day on the job, Wendy told the coordinator that the manager had made explicit sexual advances towards her. When the coordinator discussed Wendy's feelings with the manager, he countered with, "All of these young girls are alike, you smile at them and right away they misunderstand and think you are propositioning them. I'm a happily married man with four children. She's young enough to be my daughter."

Wendy was promptly removed from the job and placed in an insurance company's dead storage file office. The office had a woman manager and four work study students, plus four women in an outside office. The woman manager ran her office with military precision. Wendy called it a "sweatshop" and said the manager picked on her every day for not being able to keep up with the other three work study students. One day the manager asked Wendy about her dark color. Wendy told her that she was half Indian. The manager then began making comments about Wendy's slowness being due to her Indian heritage. Wendy was quickly removed from that situation and then refused to try any other secretarial/clerical jobs. She went to work in a fast-food restaurant working the grill and slicing tomatoes, onions, etc., in the back room. She felt that this also was a pressure situation and was not happy in this job. In her senior year of high school, she went to work for a woman who was an invalid and spent five afternoons a week cleaning, cooking, washing, and caring for this woman.

Upon the high school graduation, she placed an advertisement in a local paper offering to clean, cook, and wash for people. She started her own business cleaning houses five to six days a week. In addition, she married a factory worker (who packs boxes) and moved out of her father's house and into an attic apartment in a two-family house. She is still cleaning houses and caring for sick people. She is planning to have a child in the near future.

CAST STUDY QUESTIONS: Wendy

1. What other occupations do you think would be suitable for Wendy?

   Name at least 4 occupations.

   1. ____________________ 3. ____________________

   2. ____________________ 4. ____________________

2. Explain and discuss your rationale for selecting each occupation.

   1. ____

   ____

   2. ____

   ____

   3. ____

   ____

4. ______________________________

____

3. What would be the ideal educational program for Wendy, assuming she has been placed in a work study program leading to one of the above occupations?

____

____

____

____

____

____

4. What kind of ancillary services would you consider important to Wendy's maximum career development?

____

____

____

____

5. What do you consider to be the key element in making a successful match between Wendy and any employer?

____

6. What kind of follow-up should you use with a work study student who has experienced sexual harrassment on the job?

____

____

____

7. Is there any way to avoid bad experiences when placing a student?

____ Yes____ No

Explain. ______________________________________

____

8. Wendy eventually started her own business. Was there any indication of her ability to work independently while she was in school? Could her free enterprise spirit have been fostered by the school? Discuss.

____

____

____

____

9. Would you have made the same placement for Wendy as those described in this case study?

____ Yes ____ No

Explain. ______________________________________

____

____

REFERENCES

Gardner, P.L. Editorial: Monstrabat Viam . . . "He showed the way . . ." *Career Education Quarterly, II(4):*2-3, Fall, 1977.

Gardner, P.L. Employment of Handicapped Persons: A Survey of Characteristics and Opinions of Supervision from Small Urban Manufacturing Firms. Unpublished doctoral dissertation, Boston University, 1981.

Cushing, David. Teacher retreads: Can they make it in training? *Training/HRD,* 31-33. August 1980,

CHAPTER 7

PLANNING AND MONITORING IVEPS

Scott's homework was a mess! As the weeks went by, it became obvious to Mr. Brown, his shop teacher, that he was having increasing difficulty keeping up with the assigned readings and immense difficulty with the examinations in related instruction. If Mr. Brown asked him what he was doing in the "hands on" part of the program, Scott could answer correctly. Moreover, his shop project was progressing well, at least up to minimum standard for a *C* in the course. Frankly, Mr. Brown was baffled by Scott's erratic performance. Finally, in desperation, Mr. Brown went to the guidance department. Here he was informed that Scott had a serious reading problem and that the text materials were probably at too high a reading level for him. "What do I do now," murmured Mr. Brown.

In a school system that has developed a program of services and individualized education programs (IEPs), such a scenario is unlikely. Nevertheless, it is all too familiar in many school systems despite the new legislation on education of handicapped and disadvantaged students. While the law does not require IEPs for disadvantaged students, it is our contention that the IEP system offers an excellent methodology for preventing such scenes as the one depicted above. More important, an effective individualized vocational program (IVEP) offers the vocational teacher a built-in support system so that he/she can adequately teach Scott the skills needed for competitive employment *without* detracting from the educational program of other students.

How the IVEP Helps the Vocational Teacher

The advantages for the teacher of having an IVEP system for learning handicapped and disadvantaged students in career/vocational education are multifold. First, the vocational teacher will know what the student's strengths and weaknesses are so that he can teach to the student's strengths and make provisions for areas that need special attention. For instance, if Scott is having difficulty with the vocabulary or technical language of the trade area, the vocational teacher may want to ask for help from a reading teacher and/or ask that self-paced learning packages be purchased and made available for the student. If Scott appears to be having some difficulty learning from the overheads used in class lectures, Mr. Brown may want to give copies of the overheads to Scott and/or give copies to the resource room teacher who is helping Scott. The possibilities of providing help are myriad depending on the student and the teacher. However, those possibilities may never be recognized if Mr. Brown has not been informed of Scott's problems. Ideally, Mr. Brown would not merely be the recipient of information about Scott; he would be actively involved in the development of Scott's individualized vocational education plan. Not only would Scott's plan be more comprehensive because of Mr. Brown's involvement, but Mr. Brown would also feel some ownership in the plan and more motivation to see that it is correctly implemented.

Another important way in which the IVEP system is valuable to a shop teacher like Mr. Brown is that it gives him the chance to interact and work with the very people who can help him help Scott. In a system with adequate support personnel, the possibilities of help for Scott are restricted only by imagination and the amount of funding available. Usually, an IVEP team, that is, the group of experts assigned to develop the IVEP for a specific student, may consist of a school psychologist, a counselor, a social worker, medical personnel, and former teachers. Each of these professionals and others, e.g. a reading specialist, contribute to the diagnosis of Scott's vocational education problems and make suggestions for remediation. They also represent the kind of specialized help that is available to help Scott make it in this trade area. In schools where we have worked as consultants, we have found that the most significant outcome of the IVEP process is the increased communication between vocational educators and support personnel. When specialists began to work closely with vocational teachers for the benefit of an individual student who is having difficulty, the problem no longer seems so insurmountable to the vocational teacher or to the student. In addition, the specialist begins to pick up the technical language of the vocational teacher and gains a better understanding and respect for vocational education. The vocational teacher, in turn, acquires new teaching methods that he/she can apply in similar situations with other students. Everbody seems to win.

In becoming involved in the development of an IVEP for Scott, Mr. Brown also can become directly involved in the establishment of both short-term and long-term career goals for him. He can help determine the type of aid that will be required to support the academic side of Scott's vocational program and can help the counselors in determining the type of vocational counseling Scott will need to make it in competitive employment. He will be a key factor in helping Scott decide just what entry-level job to aim for in the short run. He can also help Scott set long-range career goals beyond the first job. The vocational teacher can help to detail the *specific* academic and vocational competencies that Scott will need to acquire to master his chosen trade area. At this point, then, the vocational teacher has the opportunity to see that Scott receives all the necessary support service that will ensure that Scott has his best shot at acquiring these voctional competencies.

The IVEP conference also offers the vocational teacher the opportunity to ask for any special equipment or services he/she feels are necessary for the appropriate vocational education of the student. If special curriculum materials or equipment are necessary for Scott's success, the IVEP system opens the door for their acquisition by the vocational teacher.

Finally, the involvement of vocational teachers in the IVEP system offers all parties concerned the opportunity to study and evaluate the *reasons* why Scott has been placed in a particular shop or trade. By understanding the rationale behind the IVEP, the vocational teacher is less likely to feel "dumped on."

IEPs and IVEPs

What is an IEP?

The Individualized Education Program (IEP) is a term that represents the currently accepted approach to implementing The Education for All Handicapped Children Act passed by Congress in 1975 (P.L. 94-142). The purpose of the act is to assure that

> all handicapped children have available to them . . . a free appropriate public education which emphasizes special education and related services designed to meet their unique needs, to assure that the rights of the handicapped children and their parents or guardians are protected, to assist States and localities to provide the education of all handicapped children, and to assess and assure the effectiveness of efforts to educate handicapped children. (P.L. 94-142, Section 601, c)

One of the major provisions of the act requires all local schools to establish (or revise) individual education plans for each handicapped child once a year and to evaluate and review each plan periodically. There must be at least one review per year, but some school districts may do it more frequently. The act also specifies that the Individualized Education Program (IEP) must include the following in written form:

1. A DESCRIPTION OF THE INDIVIDUAL STUDENT'S CURRENT EDUCATIONAL PERFORMANCE LEVELS IN SUBJECTS SUCH AS READING, MATH, ETC.
2. A LIST OF SPECIFIC GOALS AND SHORT-TERM OBJECTIVES FOR THE STUDENT.
3. A DESCRIPTION OF SPECIFIC EDUCATIONAL SERVICES WHICH WILL BE PROVIDED IN ORDER TO MEET THE GOALS AND OBJECTIVES.
4. A DESCRIPTION OF THE EXTENT TO WHICH THE STUDENT WILL PARTICIPATE IN REGULAR EDUCATION PROGRAMS.
5. A TIME PLAN FOR THE STUDENT: SPECIFIC DATE(S) FOR THE INITIATION OF THE IEP AND PROJECTED DURATION OF SERVICES.
6. AN APPROPRIATE EVALUATION MUST BE DESCRIBED. IT MUST INCLUDE (1) THE OBJECTIVE CRITERIA WHICH WILL BE USED TO DETERMINE WHETHER OR NOT THE CHILD HAS MET THE INSTRUCTIONAL OBJECTIVES AND (2) THE LEVEL OF THE ACHIEVEMENT EXPECTED. EVALUATION MUST OCCUR AT LEAST ONCE A YEAR.

It is our hypotheses that the concept of Individualized Education Programs will be extended to all children within our lifetime. This probably will occur first with court decisions about "equal opportunity" and be followed by appropriate legislation. The concept, then, of requiring educators and related personnel to tailor education to meet individual needs seems long overdue. In fact, our contention in this book is that the IEP system should be applied to disadvantaged students as well as to mildly learning handicapped students.

One note of caution: What disturbs us about the IEP system is the emphasis on the paper flow and the increasing involvement of the legal system in making "educational" and other professional decisions.

Another problem with the IEP system's emphasis on paperwork is the reality that some people just are better at paperwork than others. It is our contention that an excellent writer who has mastered the jargon of our profession can write outstanding plans for children, milk the evaluation data, and make something that is not so good look terrific. On the other hand, an outstanding program for a specific child might not pass inspection because the person writing the program/evaluation is not very good at writing. The reality of the IEP process is that it ultimately rests on the good faith of those involved. If programs are run by paper pushers who are more interested in the paper flow than the education of the child, then we are wasting our time. On the other hand, if the emphasis is on providing the best program for the child, then it is well worth the time and expense. It certainly will cost less in the long run to prepare students for a productive adult life than to pay for their upkeep on welfare or in jail or other institutions. A cost-benefit analysis will show this to be true every time.

What is an IVEP?

The Vocational Education Amendments of 1976 require

> educators to look at each person as an individual. It encourages educators to use their imagination and creativity to meet the special and unique learning needs of youth and adults with academic or economic handicaps and mental or physical disabilities which prevent them from succeeding in the regular vocational education programs. (RESURGE, '79, preface)

The act does not require that vocational educators write IEPs for disadvantaged students. It is our contention that IEPs should become the vehicle for "meeting the special and unique learning needs" of disadvantaged students as well as learning handicapped students. The logic is clear. If the IEP system works for learning handicapped students, it should work equally well for disadvantaged students who are having problems succeeding in regular vocational education programs. We call this approach the Individualized Vocational Education Program system. Our first point in defining what we mean by IVEPs is that they are applicable to all students having problems succeeding in regular vocational educational programs.

Our second point about Individualized Vocational Education

Programs is one of emphasis in the plan for each student. The emphasis in the student's plan for it to be considered an IVEP rather than an IEP should be on the *vocational* aspects of the plan. The primary focus of the IVEP, including the goals that have to do with academics, should be on preparing the student for the world of work. The vocational part of an IVEP should be the focal point for developing all short- and long-term academic or career goals. An IEP that has an "add on" page with generalized vocational goals does not fit our definition of an IVEP.

Last, we are focusing in this chapter on a specific age grouping and program assignment. IVEPs are for students in secondary or postsecondary vocational programs that are state/federal approved.

Writing an IVEP

Individualized Vocational Education Programs can be fairly simple or quite detailed and complex. IVEPs will vary from simple to complex depending upon the following conditions: (1) the needs of the student,(2) the amount of assessment required (educational, medical, psychological, vocational), (3) the policies of the particular state/local education agency, and (4) the sophistication of the team members and the writer(s) of the IVEP. Our motto is "Keep it simple!" Remember the parent/guardian and recipient of the services should be able to understand it as well as those who are charged with its implementation.

The IVEP process usually occurs when someone spots a learning problem (or other problem) in a particular student and refers the problem to the school administration. At this point a decision may or may not be made to proceed with the assessment of the student. This will depend upon the apparent seriousness of the problem. Our philosophy is that unless the educational problem is obviously a serious one, just good old common sense might solve it at an informal level. Teachers, principals, counselors, etc., have a long history of dealing with school problems without excessive use of personnel time, the costs of specialists, testing, and unneeded paperwork. Thus our recommendation at referral time is to treat the problem initially as one that can be handled by the normal methods. For instance, we know of a case where a student was referred by a classroom teacher as being retarded. It seems that this student wouldn't pay attention and didn't do his work. Instead he daydreamed and drew cartoons. He was not disruptive or unlikeable, just politely forgetful. His mother's diagnosis was boredom. He was subsequently placed in a more challenging situation. Today he is a successful trial attorney.

There are occasions, however, where the teacher has tried several strategies without success or where the teacher does not feel capable of dealing with the student's problem. This is typified in our example of Mr. Brown and Scott. Let's assume that Mr. Brown refers Scott through the appropriate channels. Mr. Brown and an administrator discuss Scott's problem and decide that it warrants the development of an IVEP for him. The next step is for the administrator who is responsible for the IVEP system to choose a team and a chairperson.

The selection of the team is probably the most critical stage in the development of an IVEP, since the content undoubtedly will be determined by the individuals selected to develop the program. At the minimum, the IVEP team should consist of –

1. a school representative (usually the chairperson)
2. the teacher involved
3. the parent or guardian
4. the student, where appropriate.

In reality, the team may be larger and can involve a variety of specialists depending on the severity of the problem. The team may also include one or more of the following specialists in addition to the people listed above:

5. school psychologist.
6. clinical psychologist/psychiatrist.
7. physician or nurse.
8. neurologist.
9. audiologist.
10. speech therapist.
11. reading specialist.
12. vocational rehabilitation counselor.
13. guidance counselor.
14. etc.

In some cases the involvement of a large multidisciplinary team in the design of a specific program may be warranted and beneficial to the student.

However, the larger the team, the more hours and expense involved. Moreover, the larger the team, the more likely there will be disagreement and delay in the decision-making process. Again, we stand by our rule of thumb: "Keep it simple." Many school districts have hired specialists who do nothing but chair IEP or IVEP teams. We recommend this approach. An experienced chairperson can avoid the tendency to "make a log out of a straw" and as time goes by can increasingly draw on experience to help facilitate the process.

The critical personnel in the IVEP process are the teachers. Since teachers are the professionals charged with implementing the plan, they must play an active and major part in the planning. Common sense as well as the literature on motivation underscores the need for the teachers to be involved. Unless they are part of the planning, they simply won't have anything invested in the success of the plan.

In developing IVEPs the vocational teacher *must* be the key factor in the multidisciplinary team. In our opinion, he/she should be responsible for the development of the career/vocational long-range goals and short-term objectives for the student. In addition, he or she should serve as the major consultant with the team for ensuring that the "academic" and other portions of the IVEP are aimed at helping the student succeed in the vocational program. Above all, the IVEP development process must be aimed at getting the vocational teacher together in a cooperative working relationship with the support personnel who are assigned to the student. No one should expect a vocational teacher to assume the total responsibility for the student's vocational education program without appropriate support services. We know of one vocational high school where support personnel specialize in working with several trade areas. This approach, in our opinion, makes for an optimal program for each student.

The IEP process as mandated by P.L. 94-142 is well documented by many other authors; therefore, this text will not belabor the subject by reviewing the steps again. We would like, however, to present an adaptation of the process for disadvantaged students. Our IVEP model for disadvantaged students adheres to the format for handicapped students in many ways such as the absolute necessity for parental consent and involvement.

The following pages are a suggested IVEP format. Individual schools, of course, vary in the format used. This model is currently being field-tested in a New England vocational school and was developed in consultation with the vocational director. The intent of the series of forms is to illustrate how such a system might work. Note that the length of the final written IVEP can vary and that the number of pages can vary according to the case. We have included illustrations where appropriate for clarification. Our motto, to repeat, is "Keep it simple."

Step 1 The teacher observes that student is having more than the usual amount of trouble in class and unsuccessfully tries several "tried and true" strategies to help the student improve.

Step 2 The teacher refers the student to the appropriate administrator or study team with brief written statements describing the student's problem. See sample referral form on page 162.

Step 3 The administrator checks with the Special Education Office (or Guidance) to see if the student is already being serviced under P.L. 94-142. If yes, is there a vocational element to the IEP? If no, the administrator checks to see if the student can be categorized as disadvantaged. See the sample referral form on page 163.

Step 4 The teacher meets with the administrator and/or study team to discuss the student, and a decision is made to try different intervention techniques or to refer the student for evaluation. See the sample notice of meetings on page 164.

Step 5 If the student is referred for evaluation, administrator or team leader makes contact with the parents to discuss the situation, to explain the evaluation process and permission forms. See sample letter on page 165.

Step 6 Appropriate evaluations conducted. See sample forms on pages 168-170.

Step 7 Meeting with IVEP team and parents and student, if appropriate, to develop the IVEP. See sample programs on pages 166-167, 171-175.

Figure 27. Suggested IVEP process for disadvantaged students.

Notes on Developing Your Own IVEP System

1. Get the vocational teacher who will be responsible for implementation involved early in the game. The best, most well thought out IVEP is worthless unless the implementor is committed and involved.
2. Familiarize yourself with state and federal regulations. Make certain your procedures meet these criteria. It may be helpful to seek consultation from a State Department of Education official.
3. Use as few forms as possible. Try a pilot run or two on your paper system. Consolidate and simplify. Don't get hung up on filling out every form for every IVEP and filling up the blank space. Teachers do not like excessive paperwork. (Does anyone?)
4. Don't get caught up in the paper flow process. Generating reports

and excessive documentation at the expense of providing services to individual students is an easy trap to fall into. Demonstrate competence with quality individualized programs and not with undue attention to size and format of the report. Our rule of thumb is that the quality of most reports, including IVEPs, is usually inversely related to the length of the report and the amount of professional jargonese.

Notes on the Letter to Parents

1. Please call the parent before sending anything home. This can be a frightening and demeaning process for many parents. Take time to explain the process *fully*. You will have done it so many times that it is easy to take things for granted. This is more than likely the first time for many parents and they have no idea what you are talking about. Many parents feel that the idea of "special help" has punitive connotations. They need much reassurance from you that you want their son or daughter to succeed in school as much as they do and that this will help. Explain what the evaluation consists of in *lay terms*.
2. Have the letter personally typed. Bureaucratic photocopied form letters are insensitive and inexcusable. The parents will be upset enough. If you truly want helpful parents, show them respect.
3. Eliminate as much jargon from the letter as possible. The word *evaluation* is enough to scare the daylights out of many parents. You will certainly want to explain their rights as parents during the telephone conversation, and you may want to include information about parent rights as part of the mailing package.
4. You may need bilingual versions of the letter and forms if you are dealing with non-English-speaking parents. Also plan on having a translator at the meeting to ensure that parents really understand what is happening.

INDIVIDUAL VOCATIONAL EDUCATION PROGRAM
REFERRAL FORM

The following student is experiencing difficulty in his/her vocational program.

Name of Student ______________________________

Class: ________Freshman; ________Sophomore; ________Junior; ________Senior

Vocational program ______________________________

Reason for referral:

____academic problem
comments: ______________________________
____
____

____performance problem
comments: ______________________________
____
____

____behavior problem
comments: ______________________________
____
____

____attendance problem
comments: ______________________________
____
____

____other problem
comments: ______________________________
____
____

Submitted to Vocational Office by: ______________________________

Date ____________________

Sample Referral Form

TO: Special Education Office DATE:

FROM: Vocational Office

SUBJECT: REFERRAL

The following student has been referred to the Vocational Office as not succeeding in his/her vocational program. We are presently in the process of organizing a team meeting to investigate the need for support services for this student. Would you please check your file for information on this student that might assist us.

Student name ________________________________

Class: ___Freshman; ___Sophomore; ___Junior; ___Senior

Address: ________________________________

____

TO BE FILLED OUT BY GUIDANCE OFFICE:

This student is handicapped: ____yes; ____ no

This student is getting support services through Special Education: _____ yes; _____ no

This student has an IEP: _____ yes; _____ no

If yes, there is a vocational addendum: _____ yes; _____no

If yes, please submit a copy to the Vocational Office.

____
Signature of Guidance Representative

____
Date

Thank you for your assistance. Please return this form to the Vocational Office.

INDIVIDUAL VOCATIONAL EDUCATION PROGRAM

TO: ______________________ (Teacher making referral)

FROM: ______________________

DATE: ______________________

SUBJECT: ______________________ (name of student referred)

The above student is not receiving any support services at this time. We are organizing a team to review the student's progress and to investigate the need for support services.

A meeting will be held:

Day and Date:

Time:

Place:

Please come prepared to discuss the student's progress in your course in terms of academic achievement, performance abilities, behavior, attendance, and any other points you consider relevant.

SAMPLE LETTER TO PARENT

Date

Mr. and Mrs. X. Smith
110 51st Street
AnyCity, ST 11111

Dear Mr. and Mrs. Smith:

I enjoyed talking with you on the telephone on Thursday. As we discussed, the Student Study Team feels that Scott may need special help to be more successful in his vocational program. We would like Scott to receive the following kinds of evaluations, which will be arranged for by the school:

When the evaluations are done, I will contact you again to ask you to come to school so that you can see the results and meet with the teachers to talk about Scott's program. If you agree that Scott needs special help, a team of teachers and other personnel will be appointed to work with you and your son to determine the things that Scott does well, where he is having trouble, and what he needs to help him learn better in school. Based on these findings, an individualized vocational education program will be designed to help ensure his success in the automotive program.

We need your written approval to have the evaluations done. Would you please sign the bottom of this letter and return it in the enclosed stamped envelope. No changes will be made in Scott's program without your approval.

I will be happy to talk with you at any time to answer any questions you may have. You can set up an appointment to come into school to see me or we can talk over the telephone. I'm looking forward to working with you.

Sincerely,

PARENTAL PERMISSION FOR EVALUATION OF ___Scott Smith___

☐ I give my permission for my child to receive the evaluations described above.

☐ I do not give my permission for my child to receive the evaluations described above.

______________________ Your name

______________________ Relationship to child

______________________ Date

INDIVIDUALIZED VOCATIONAL EDUCATION PROGRAM
XYZ SCHOOL

DATE OF REPORT ________________ THIS PLAN COVERS THE PERIOD ______TO ______

STUDENT NAME ____
LAST FIRST MIDDLE INITIAL

DATE OF BIRTH ___/___/___ AGE ___ SEX: ___MALE ___ FEMALE

VOCATIONAL PROGRAM __________________________

....

PARENT(s)/GUARDIAN (FULL NAME)

1. ____ ___PARENT ___GUARDIAN
LAST FIRST MIDDLE INITIAL

2. ____ ___PARENT ___GUARDIAN
LAST FIRST MIDDLE INITIAL

WORK PHONE _______________ HOME PHONE _________________

....

_________________________ Date of Original Referral ___/___/___
Signature of Referring Party

....

DATE(s) OF TEAM MEETINGS

___/___/___ ___/___/___

___/___/___ ___/___/___ Next Scheduled Dates:

___/___/___ ___/___/___

T E A M M E M B E R S

NAME	TITLE	ROLE/RESPONSIBILITY
______________________	Chairperson	______________________________
______________________	______________	______________________________
______________________	______________	______________________________
______________________	______________	______________________________
______________________	______________	______________________________

....

☐ Disadvantaged
Criteria: ____
____

I certify that the goals and objectives in this plan are those recommended by the Team assigned to this student and that the services recommended will be provided.

______________________________ Date: __/__/__
Signature, Vocational Director

______________________________ Date: __/__/__
Signature IVEP Team Chairperson

RECIPIENT OF SERVICES RESPONSE:

__PARENT(S) __GUARDIAN __STUDENT OVER 18

PLEASE SIGN YOUR CHOICE BELOW AND GIVE US YOUR COMMENTS IF YOU WISH.

I accept this educational plan ______________________________ Date __/__/__
Signature

I do not accept this educational plan ______________________________ Date __/__/__
Signature

I would like to postpone my decision until an independent evaluation is completed. ______________________________ Date __/__/__
Signature

INDIVIDUALIZED VOCATIONAL EDUCATION PROGRAM FOR ______________________________

RESULTS OF TESTING

I. CURRENT FUNCTIONING

ACADEMIC/RELATED ACADEMIC PROFILE

TEST	DATE	RAW SCORE	OTHER SCORE

FINDINGS/RECOMMENDATIONS (attach separate report if necessary)

VOCATIONAL PROFILE

TEST	DATE	RAW SCORE	OTHER SCORE

FINDINGS/RECOMMENDATIONS (Attach separate report if necessary)

OTHER MEDICAL/PSYCHOLOGICAL TESTING

TESTS	FINDINGS

Page ___ of ___

INDIVIDUALIZED VOCATIONAL EDUCATION PROGRAM of ________________________

I. Current Functioning

ACADEMIC/RELATED ACADEMIC SKILLS (state in behavioral terms)

____

____

____

____

____

____

____

____

AREAS FOR REMEDIATION IN ACADEMIC/RELATED ACADEMIC AREAS

____

____

____

____

____

____

Page ___ of ___

INDIVIDUALIZED VOCATIONAL EDUCATION PROGRAM of ____________________

I. CURRENT FUNCTIONING

SUMMARY OF CURRENT VOCATIONAL SKILLS (state in behavioral terms).

____

____

____

____

____

____

____

____

AREAS FOR REMEDIATION IN SHOP ACTIVITIES (state in behavioral terms).

____

____

____

____

____

____

____

____

Page ___ of ___

INDIVIDUALIZED VOCATIONAL EDUCATION PROGRAM
19__-19__

STUDENT'S NAME ____________ INSTRUCTIONAL AREA ____________ PERSON RESPONSIBLE ____________

LONG RANGE GOAL: NO ______________________________

Short-Range Objectives	Beginning Date	Estimated Completion Date	Stragegies & Materials	Evaluation Criteria and Procedures

Page ___ of ___

INDIVIDUALIZED VOCATIONAL EDUCATION PROGRAM*
AUTO BODY

DUTY AND TASK(S)	TERMINAL AND INTERIM OBJECTIVES	SUGGESTED LEARNING ACTIVITIES	SUGGESTED EVALUATION MEASURES
1) To have students demonstrate his/her knowledge acquired in removing mouldings, trim, and cleaning exterior and interior surfaces of body panels. 2) To have students understand the purpose of surface preparation. 3) To have students understand the basic principles involved in becoming a good leader.	1) The student will be able to identify moulding and trim using the terminology common to auto body repair trade. 2) The student will be able to explain why surface preparation is important if paint failures are to be avoided. 3) The student will demonstrate methods used in removing wax and grease from metal surfaces. 4) The student will be able to identify several reasons for becoming a good leader. 5) The student will be able to identify ten (10) characteristics of a good leader. 6) The student will be able to list several values related to having leadership ability.	1) Moulding and trim will be saved from a vehicle disected in a previous lesson and displayed with proper title. Each item will be discussed. 2) Students will observe a demonstration of paint being applied to a clean surface and paint being applied to an unclean surface. 3) The students will receive hands on experience in preparation of metal. 4) The students will complete a personality self-rating sheet, identify leaders within the community and discuss the relationship of the two (2) topics. 5) A discussion of values with respect, education, pride, security, etc., as topics. 6) Members of the Craft Committee will be invited in to make a presentation to the class on locating employment and individual experiences.	1) Evaluation will be concerned with matching terms to correct definitions. 2) The student will be evaluated in his/her job in metal preparation. 3) Notebooks will be evaluated. 4) Workbooks will be evaluated.

*Provided by Dr. Kenneth G. Webber, Director of Vocational Education, Portsmouth High School, Portsmouth, New Hampshire and his staff.

Page ___ of ___

INDIVIDUALIZED VOCATIONAL EDUCATION PROGRAM*
AUTO BODY

DUTY AND TASK(S)	TERMINAL AND INTERIM OBJECTIVES	SUGGESTED LEARNING ACTIVITIES	SUGGESTED EVALUATION MEASURES
Duty Statement	Terminal Objective		
Perform automotive lubrication service.	Given an Automobile requiring periodic lubrication service, the student shall inspect and replenish all lubrication points and lubricant levels on the vehicles chassis, engine, and drive train to the manufacturers specifications	Text Assignment Lecture Film Strip Demonstration Open Lab sequence	Written Test Observation Checklist
Task Statement	Interim Objectives		
1. Lubricated Chassis and Front End.	Given an Automobile requiring front end lubrication service, the student shall find, inspect, and grease the vehicles steering linkages, ball joints, and wheel bearings without overfilling the fittings.	Demonstration Open Lab sequence	Observation Checklist
Task Statements	Interim Objectives		
2. Change engine oil and filter	Given an Automobile, the student shall drain the oil, change the filter, and refill the crankcase to its proper capacity with no leaks.	Demonstration Open Lab sequence	Observation Checklist
3. Replaces fluid and filters in transmissions.	Given and Automobile with a standard transmission, the student shall drain the lubricant and refill to the proper level with the correct type of gear lube.	Demonstration Open Lab sequence	Observation Checklist

*Provided by Dr. Kenneth G. Webber, Director of Vocational Education, Portsmouth High School, Portsmouth, New Hampshire and his staff.

Page ___ of ___

INDIVIDUALIZED VOCATIONAL EDUCATION PROGRAM*
AUTO BODY

DUTY AND TASK(S)	TERMINAL AND INTERIM OBJECTIVES	SUGGESTED LEARNING ACTIVITIES	SUGGESTED EVALUATION MEASURES
	Given an Automobile with an automatic transmission, the student shall drop the cover pan, drain the fluid, replace the filter, and refill the transmission to the proper level with no leaks	Demonstration Open Lab sequence	Observation Checklist
	Interim Objectives		
Task Statements 4. Changes differential fluid	Given an Automobile, the student shall remove the differential cover plate, inspect the unit for wear, replace the cover plate, and refill the differential to its proper level with no leaks	Demonstration Open Lab sequence	Observation Checklist

*Provided by Dr. Kenneth G. Webber, Director of Vocational Education, Portsmouth High School, Portsmouth, New Hampshire and his staff.

Page ___ of ___

INDIVIDUALIZED VOCATIONAL EDUCATION PROGRAM
HOME ECONOMICS

DUTY AND TASK(S)	TERMINAL AND INTERIM OBJECTIVES	SUGGESTED LEARNING ACTIVITIES	SUGGESTED EVALUATION MEASURES
Duty Statement	Terminal Objective		
0.1 Interpreting and following a recipe	Each student when given a recipe, will identify and assemble ingredients and equipment, interpret the abbreviations used, and combine ingredients according to the outlined procedure, to successfully complete an edible product.	1) Abbreviation handout -use textbooks and cookbooks to determine meanings 2) Handout -common kitchen utensils -basic kitchen equipment 3) View Filmstrip -measuring ingredients	Pen and Paper Test Student Lab Experience - Self Evaluation - Teacher checklist
Task Statement	Interim Objectives		
1. Interpret recipe Abbreviations	Given a list of 20 abbreviations, the student will be able to identify the meaning of the abbreviated work with 100% efficiency.	4) View demonstration by Instructure -interpreting abbreviations -measuring accurately	
2. Identify and use needed equipment	Given a recipe, the student will assemble the necessary equipment and use each piece as specified in the recipe.	5) Handout -Lab kitchen diagram -location and use of utensils equipment and supplies	
3. Interpret measurements and measure accurately	Given a recipe, the student will identify the measurement, use the proper utensil and obtain an accurate measurement of each ingredient.	6) View Demonstration by Instructor -locating and using Lab kitchen utensils, equipment and supplies.	
4. Follow a logical sequence of directions	Given a recipe, the student will read, comprehend and complete the directions for assembling the finished product with 100% efficiency.	7) Instruction -Reading recipes -following directions 8) Student Lab Experience -food preparation	

*Provided by Dr. Kenneth G. Webber, Director of Vocational Education, Portsmouth High School, Portsmouth, New Hampshire and his staff.

CHAPTER 8

WHERE DO WE GO FROM HERE?

IN the previous chapters we discussed a number of ways that practitioners can address the educational and training limitations that serve as barriers to employment for handicapped and disadvantaged youth. We also illustrated some of the problems and methods for remediation associated with inappropriate attitudes that may be held by handicapped and disadvantaged students and that may prevent many of them from making an appropriate transition from school to work and from reaching their highest occupational potential. Despite the effectiveness of intervention and remediation techniques such as we have mentioned, almost any practitioner in the field will agree with us that we have a long way to go before we can state that our current human service system is meeting the needs of students such as Scott. The recent emphasis on eliminating rather than expanding governmental efforts to address the problems associated with unemployment or misemployment of handicapped and disadvantaged youth undoubtedly will slow the pace towards optimum service delivery.

Whether or not there are federal funds for career and vocational programs does not take away our responsibility for providing them. One way or the other, programs for helping handicapped and disadvantaged workers enter the mainstream of our working society must be continued. Since we do not have a crystal ball, we can offer little in terms of forecasting the financing of such endeavors in the future. What we can offer is our own ideas about what should be done programmatically to expand and upgrade appropriate career and vocational services for handicapped and disadvantaged youth.

This chapter focuses on goals for the rest of the century. It is devoted to describing what we think must be accomplished during the next two decades if we are truly to meet the career and vocational needs of the learning handicapped and disadvantaged youth in our country.

The goals in the next sections are based on a number of sources. Many of them were derived from our own experiences as teachers, work placement coordinators, university professors, project directors, and program administrators. Other goals have been derived from national and regional surveys that we have been involved in over the past decade (Beatty, Gardner & Avallon, 1981; Gardner, D., 1977; Gardner, P., 1981). In any event, whether the future goals and needs outlined herein came from hard data collected in surveys or from our own professional opinion, we offer them to you as our best estimates of appropriate starting points for planning the balance of the century. Implementation is up to you.

GOALS FOR SCHOOL PROGRAMS

1. Public and Private Schools Should Budget for a Full-time Administrator to Handle Career Education on a K Through 12 Basis

Developing and supervising programs that are effective is a full-time job. A person wearing too many hats not only is destined for career burnout but more than likely will not be able to do any of the assigned tasks well. Compare programs where the director is part-time with those under a full-time director and see the impact that a full-time person can make on program scope and quality.

2. We Must Place More Emphasis on Developing Procedures for Predicting Training and Job Success

If program directors and job placement specialists are going to be able to help handicapped and disadvantaged students select appropriate training programs and/or jobs successfully, they must not only be better trained in assessment, but they must also have available to them assessment materials and facilities as well as follow-up data. The hallmark of a quality program is an assessment center with trained personnel who work closely with program personnel in helping students choose training and jobs wisely. The predominant mode, unfortunately, is an overburdened and/or poorly trained work study coordinator who finds a job and then talks the student into taking it.

3. The Major Goal of School Programs Should be to Help Mildly Learning Handicapped and Disadvantaged Students Acquire Saleable Skills

Many practitioners, when asked on a survey we conducted, admitted that as many as 50 percent of their students are *not* ready for competitive employment. A great many others would not even make an estimate. Too often a program is judged as successful or not based on criteria such as number of students in the program, number of courses taught within the program, number of dollars received in grants, number of students graduating, etc. The bottom line, however, is that none of these things are important if the student does not leave the system with skills and is not able to sell them.

4. We Must Eliminate the Artificial Dichotomy of "Practitioners" and "Researchers" in Education

Teaching is no longer just an art form. There is a large body of knowledge on learning available to teachers, which is based on empirically tested theory. Although undergraduate students may become aware of learning theories during their training, very few are ever required to have a working knowledge of the research and evaluation that form the basis of learning theory development. It is sadder still that master's programs often require only one research course and sometimes not even that. Experienced teachers coming back to school for advanced degrees are put into methods courses that give them more of the same. Their time could be better spent learning to evaluate their current teaching methods empirically or pilot testing new approaches they would like to use in their classrooms.

Some common refrains are "I'm not interested in that theoretical or statistical stuff. I want to relate to the kids"; or "I'm a practitioner. I don't need to read research articles." Teachers who espouse these philosophies have no understanding or appreciation of the contribution that research can make to their ability to relate to the kids or simply to teach.

One teacher we know, who spent endless hours developing a very creative game for special needs students to help them learn the vocabulary associated with the driver's test, decided to evaluate the effectiveness of the game as part of a research methods course she was taking. She randomly assigned students in her class to either the game or to flash cards. She fully expected that the game would be shown to be much more effective and had all sorts of visions about marketing the game through Milton Bradley or an equally large company and making lots of money. What she found through her evaluation was that the students learned more words through the use of flash cards! Does this mean that she should not use games any more? Of course not. The students loved them and she really enjoys making them. What did she learn from the evaluation? She learned that the games were not the best way to *teach* vocabulary but that they could be used very effectively as a reinforcement device. The more efficient approach was to have the student learn the words through flash cards. Once they had reached a specific criterion, they could use the game. The game then served as a double reinforcer — it reinforced the vocabulary words, and it reinforced the students' efforts to achieve criterion.

We have great respect for the clinical hunches of experienced teachers, but this story illustrates that those hunches are sometimes clouded by personal prejudices. The teacher in our story was absolutely convinced that the game was the most effective approach to help students learn vocabulary. Her judgment was influenced by her enjoyment in developing the games and her students' enjoyment in playing them. An objective evaluation helped to put the game into a better perspective — one that was actually of more benefit to the students.

If we are to keep up with modern technology, we must put more emphasis on applying current research findings and methods in the classroom. We must also put more emphasis on encouraging practitioners to become researchers.

5. We Must Place Greater Emphasis on Monitoring Program Outcomes and Refining Programs to Meet Changing Needs

It has almost become a clichè to say that we live in an ever-changing, highly technological society in which one can very quickly become outdated. It is a fact, however, and schools must learn to follow up on their graduates and to use the findings of these follow-up studies to improve and refine existing programs and to develop new programs.

One caveat we want to mention here is that a poorly designed follow-up study is not much better than no follow-up study. Inadequate return rates and poorly written questions can combine to give a misleading view of the real situation. The error of this warped picture is further compounded by decisions based on the results of the "findings" of the survey. Chapter 6 contains some hints for surveys and some references. Another excellent reference for anyone conducting surveys is *Mail and Telephone Surveys: The Total Design Method* by Dillman (1978).

6. We Must Place More Emphasis on Using Advisory Committees for Career/Vocational Education Programs

It is a well-known but unwritten fact that most advisory committees in education are paper committees. The time has come for us to accept that we can learn a lot from practitioners in the competitive sector of the economy. Properly utilized advisory committees can help refine the vocational curriculum and *keep it up to date.* Committee members can help find jobs for students and lend support to proposed program changes.

The private sector can also be a source of funding. Many an innovative programmer has found funding from private enterprise when the government till came up empty. One very creative administrator decided that some of the students could profit from a service station attendant's program. He had difficulty getting federal or state funds for the program, so he decided to go to private industry. He got clearance from the superintendent for a special telephone budget and proceeded to call the headquarters of all the major oil companies in the country. In this process, he discovered that a major oil company had a program that sounded very much like what he wanted. He called the company, found out the criteria for funding, and started to build his case. The oil company flew someone out to talk to the administrator and subsequently agreed to fund the program. They put a teacher from the school through their training program during the summer, donated all necessary equipment to the school, including all sorts of training materials such as overhead projectors, slide tapes, and simulation packages. In addition, the company provided cooperative jobs for the students by subsidizing the salaries of students who were given jobs by local dealers. It was hoped that the service stations would keep the students on as regular employees after graduation, but there was no obligation to do so. In return for this support, the school had to agree to pay the salary of the instructor and to keep the program going after the first year. The service station attendant's course became an excellent program and served a number of handicapped and disadvantaged students.

GOALS FOR FEDERAL AND STATE AGENCIES

1. Federal and State Agencies Must Increase Funding of Career/Vocational Programs for Handicapped and Disadvantaged Youth

In these times of Reaganomics, budget cuts, school closings, and layoffs, it may sound rather idealistic for us to call on state and federal government to increase funding of vocational education programs. In point of fact, there is a *strong economic argument* for funding such programs. If we do not train our youth for gainful employment, if we do not provide them with an opportunity to share in the benefits of our capitalistic society, if we do not give them a chance to develop into contributing citizens, then we as taxpayers will continue to underwrite the costs of not doing so. We maintain that these costs are substantially more than the educational costs of training our youth for work. The costs of not training can be estimated as a sizable proportion of the federal and state monies expended on prisons, crime prevention and losses, welfare, food stamps, and other assorted human services that we daily provide to chronically underemployed and unemployed youth and adults who do not have salable skills.

2. Federal and State Agencies Must Require That all Funded Programs be Evaluated Professionally at Least Once a Year

Let's face it, the American taxpayer is fed up with paying top dollar for ineffective programs. The only way we know how to ensure that vocational programs live up to their promises is to have them monitored by third-party evaluators with professional evaluation skills. The advantages are twofold: (1) Sound evaluations can either demonstrate the viability of a program and ensure continued funding at adequate levels or lend support for the elimination of wasteful and ineffective ones, and (2) a good evaluation always offers program administrators suggestions for improvement of the delivery of services.

3. Federal and State Agencies Must Insist That all Vocational Programs Provide Quality Guidance and Placement Services as an Integral Part of the Program

Typically, placement services take a back seat to training. In most school systems such services are either inadequate or nonexistent. Job placement ranks near the bottom of the school's priority list even though good placement is critical to the successful transition from school to work for most mildly learning handicapped and disadvantaged youth.

A corollary to good placement services is good career guidance. Guidance counselors are often charged with spending too much time with the students headed to college at the expense of those who will enter the labor force directly. Counselor education needs to place more emphasis on training counselors to help students, college bound or not, to make wise career choices, to know how to present themselves properly in an interview, and to acquire appropriate job search skills. Good career guidance does not have to be an expensive proposition when counselors are properly trained and have access to supplementary materials and computer guidance systems. Students who have effective career guidance are less likely to experience difficulty in choosing a career or job and in making the critical transition from school to work.

GOALS FOR COLLEGES AND UNIVERSITIES

1. Every Teacher of Every Subject Should be Required to Complete a Training Program in Career Development Education

Universities and colleges should collaborate with state agencies to ensure that every teacher has had training in career development education. A basic understanding of the relationship between the career development of a child and young adult and the development and enhancement of the child or adolescent's self-concept is a must for every educator. Teachers need to understand that each of us shares the responsibility for helping the student grow into a productive adult. Moreover, teachers must recognize that an essential element of obtaining a satisfactory adult adjustment is the degree to which the adults' career development can be classified.

2. Colleges and Universities who Train Teachers, Counselors, and Other Educational Personnel to Work in the Field of Career and Vocational Education Should Require that They Acquire In-depth Work Experience in Competitive Employment

Our experience (and the hard data from our surveys) supports the idea that teachers and others working in the field should have competitive employment work experience. Most practitioners have less than five years' business experience and over half have less than two years'. Without a real grasp of the world of work, especially in more responsible positions (many practitioners have had business experience at the entry level only), it is obvious that many do not truly understand the problems of business people or their real needs. Without understanding, it is difficult for real collaboration to take place between school programs and the business community.

3. University and College Schools of Education Should Require a New Emphasis in Training Teachers and Other Educational Personnel in Program Evaluation

As we mentioned earlier in this chapter, the American taxpayer has passed the point where he is willing to pay for programs that cannot show progress towards desirable goals. Our experience is that most teacher training programs de-emphasize educational research, evaluation, and statistics. We have a profession comprised of personnel who are either ignorant about, inadequately trained in, or just plain turned off by the knowledge in their field that separates the scientific study of education from education as an art form. The result is that 90 percent or more of our practitioners haven't the least notion of how to design an educational evaluation or how to interpret one or how to use the data collected to improve their own programs. This rejection of education as a "science" permeates the field from entry level to doctoral programs.

4. Teacher Training Programs Should Actively Recruit Females to Work in Career and Vocational Education for Mildly Learning Handicapped and Disadvantaged Youth

This recommendation is based on the obvious. Most vocational educators are males. Such a condition continues to reinforce sex stereotyping in occupations.

5. Schools of Education Should use Their Expertise to Develop a Wide Variety of Curriculum Materials for Target Populations

Universities and colleges that have research and development programs should concentrate on helping the practitioners in the field develop, field-test, and refine curriculum materials that use the latest in our educational technology to help learning handicapped and disadvantaged students master their chosen occupation rapidly and effectively.

A GOAL FOR EVERYONE

Teachers, Counselors, Parents, Employers, and Other Interested Parties Must be Given a Better Understanding of Importance of Attitudes to the Successful Employment of Learning Handicapped and Disadvantaged Youth

The emphasis in most educational programs is on having students obtain academic skills. In vocational programs, the mastery of specific vocational skills carries equal weight. While the mastery of basic academic and vocational skills is, without question, important, there is not enough attention given to the development of an effective work personality. Teachers and others need to work on helping students acquire the appropriate attitudes for job success. Moreover, more attention should be given to helping teachers, employers, and other professionals and parents gain increased knowledge of the work potential of learning handicapped and disadvantaged youth. Teachers, students, and employers need to learn that at least half of the battle for success in the work place is related directly to one's attitudes and expectations. If you don't think you can succeed, the chances are that you won't. If you don't believe in your student or if the student doesn't believe in himself, what can you expect?

REFERENCES

Beatty, G.J., Gardner, D.C. & Avallon, J.L. National survey of the training needs of secondary regular class teachers for working with handicapped students. *College Student Journal, 15(3),* Fall, 1981.

Gardner, D.C. Survey of career education for the handicapped in the six New England states. Boston, MA: Boston University School of Education. Final Report: Project RETOOL (University of Alabama) USOE Grant #G007501369, 1977 ERIC ED 150 306.

Gardner, P.L. Employment of handicapped persons: A survey of characteristics and opinions of supervisors from small urban manufacturing firms. Unpublished doctoral dissertation, Boston University, 1981.

APPENDIX A

MEASURES OF LOCUS OF CONTROL AND CAREER MATURITY

CAREER MATURITY INVENTORY

CRITES'S Career Maturity Inventory (1973) was developed as a heuristic model for research purposes. It was based on Ginzberg, Ginzburg, Axelrod, and Herma's notion that "the choice of an occupation is a process, not simply a one-time event which . . . progresses through differentiable periods of deliberation culminating in a more or less satisfactory and satisfying compromise between personal needs and occupational realities" (1951).

The Career Maturity Inventory (CMI) has two parts. Part I is the Attitude Scale. Part II consists of five Competence Tests. The CMI has no total score; thus, all research on the scale involves separate scales for each subtest. The scores are interrelated, however. Wilton (1978) factor analyzed the Attitude Scale and four of the five subtests and found that they loaded onto one factor. Unfortunately, Wilton (1978) did not use Competence Test 5.

Reliability

A test-retest reliability coefficient of .71 for 1,648 students in grades six through twelve and an average internal consistency by grade of .74 (Kuder-Richardson Formula 20) for the Attitude Scale is reported by Crites (1973). Reliability of the Competence Tests was demonstrated by internal consistency coefficients ranging from .72 to .90 with two exceptions.

Validity

Validity measures on the Competence Tests were done in 1973. Studies on construct validity found that in most grades the Occupational Information, Goal Selection, and Planning subtests have the highest intercorrelations (.60). All intercorrelations were significant at or beyond the .01 level (Crites, 1973).

DIFFERENT SITUATIONS INVENTORY

The Different Situations Inventory (DSI) (Gardner & Warren, 1978) is a locus of control measure consisting of two separate scales: (1) the Self Report form and, (2) the Rater form. Both forms have identical items. However, the directions for the Self Report form ask a person to estimate how he or she would respond in a given situation. The directions for the Rater form ask a Rater (a person familiar with the person being rated) to estimate how he or she thinks the subject being rated would respond in given situations. The DSI consists of twenty items; the form is forced choice and is scored in the direction of internality.

Reliability

Ifenwanta (1978) found a test-retest reliability coefficient of .90 for the Self Report form. Using an "item difficulty and discrimination" approach, he reports that the DSI was "strongly discriminative between the upper and lower median groups." Ifenwanta (1978) computed point biserial coefficients of correlation between each item and the total score. Using the Guilford and Fruchter (1978) formula to determine acceptable item to total score correlations, it was found to be r = .22. He concluded that the DSI was "a very reliable instrument with about 85% of the test items significantly correlated to the total score" (p. 52) (see Table II).

TABLE II
Point Biserial Correlations, Item-Total Score Analysis
Different Situations Inventory
Self Report From (N = 40)*

Item	r	Item	r
1.	.24	11.	.16
2.	.43	12.	.31
3.	.25	13.	.09
4.	.35	14.	.27
5.	.32	15.	.26
6.	.45	16.	.46
7.	.45	17.	.48
8.	.26	18.	.35
9.	.57	19.	.28
10.	.51	20.	.01

*From Ifenwanta, 1978, p. 88.

In a study using the Rater form, Wilton (1978) found an interrater reliability coefficient of .673 (Cronback Alpha) for three ratings on each subject (N = 182). He reports that when ratings were reduced to twenty averages and adjusted for missing data, the internal consistency coefficient was .856 (p. 27).

Population Statistics

The DSI is still in the experimental stage, and norms for various subgroups have not yet been established. Tables III and IV report means and standard deviations of various populations on both the Self Report form and the Rater form.

Validity

Content validity was addressed during the development of the instrument. Content selection was determined by comparing items to typical items in locus of control measures already published. An equal number of items were written for each of our subconstruct categories (1) independence/dependence, (2) other-directed/inner-directed; (3) skill/chance and (4) responsible/not responsible. The items were submitted to three judges who had published research on locus of control. They were asked to label responses as "internal" or "external" independently. The judges were in 100 percent agreement with each other and the authors on every item.

Ifenwanta (1978) found a high significant correlation between Rotter's I-E scale and the DSI Self Report form (r = .66, p = .01, N = 40). As predicted using the DSI Self Report, Arrangio (1981) found that degree of alienation was inversely related to internal locus of control (r = -.32, p = $<$001). Gardner, Beatty & Bigelow (1981) found that the DSI Self Report correlated significantly with the Work Situations Inventory (WSI) (Gardner, Beatty & Kurtz, 1980) (r = .56, p = .01, N = 48). The WSI is a locus of control measure designed to measure locus of control in work situations only.

The DSI Rater form has been reported to correlate significantly with the Nowicki-Strickland Locus of Control Scale (von Esch, 1978; Wilton, 1978) and the James Locus of Control Scale (von Esch, 1978).

In addition to data on criterion-related validity on both forms

TABLE III
Means, Standard Deviations of Selected Group on Self Report Form
Different Situations Inventory

Population	N	Mean	Standard Deviation	Reference
Junior College Women	69	14.58	2.15	Cowan, 1979
Male and Female High School Students Pretreatment, experimental	22	14.14	2.45	Grossman, 1979
Male and Female High School Students Pretreatment, control	16	13.62	3.59	Grossman, 1979
Male and Female Nigerian College Students in the USA	40	15.23	2.68	Ifenwanta, 1978
Compensatory College Freshmen, Experimental (After treatment)	24	16.16	2.75	Curry, 1980
Compensatory College Freshmen, Experimental (After treatment)	25	15.56	1.98	Curry, 1980
Compensatory College Freshmen (Control)	25	13.48	2.14	Curry, 1980
High School Students After treatment, Experimental	24	16.1	2.1	Gardner, Beatty, Bigelow, 1981
High School Students Control	24	13.4	3.4	Gardner, Beatty, Bigelow, 1980
High School Students After treatment, Experimental	25	16.4	2.34	Bigelow, in review
High School Students Control	25	14.4	3.35	Bigelow, in review
High School Students Pretreatment, experimental	25	13.80	2.21	Bigelow, 1981
High School Students Pretreatment, experimental	25	14.25	2.97	Bigelow, 1981
High School Students Pretreatment, control	25	13.40	3.68	Bigelow, 1981
High School Students After treatment, experimental	25	13.95	2.86	Bigelow, 1981
High School Students After treatment, experimental	25	16.05	2.44	Bigelow, 1981
High School Students After treatment, control	25	13.75	3.67	Bigelow, 1981

TABLE IV
Means, Standard Deviations of Selected Group on Rater Form
Different Situations Inventory

Population	N	Mean	Standard Deviation	Reference
Trainable Retarded Adults	63	7.22	2.96	Carmody, 1980
Black and Hispanic CETA Program Adults	74	8.04	4.61	von Esch, 1978
Junior College Women	69	11.01	3.66	Cowan, 1979

above, several studies suggest that the DSI has good construct validity. Predicting from social learning theory (Rotter, 1966), several researchers report significant correlations between both forms of the DSI and various measures of career maturity. These are discussed later.

Another test of construct validity involves the study of the theoretical relationship between locus of control and achievement. One can predict that persons who have an internal locus of control should be the "achievers." Little research on the DSI has been done in this area. However, those studies which have been done are consistent with theory and work on other locus of control scales. Von Esch (1978) reports that the Rater form of the DSI discriminated between low and high achievers in training programs of CETA workers. He also cites an unpublished study by Gardner and Kurtz in which they report a significant correlation between the DSI Self Report form and grade point average of female college students.

Theorists on change techniques of locus of control orientation (e.g. MacDonald, 1972; Gardner & Gardner, 1974; Gardner & Warren, 1978a; Gardner & Beatty, 1980) propose that certain theoretically based instructional/counseling procedures can change a person's locus of control. Seven studies on the DSI Self Report form found significant increases in "internality" of students who received these theoretically based treatments (Arrangio, 1981; Beatty & Gardner, 1979; Bigelow, in review; Bigelow, 1981; Curry, 1980; Gardner, Beatty & Bigelow, 1981; Reilly, 1981).

WORK SITUATIONS INVENTORY

The Work Situations Inventory (WSI) was developed on the notion that it would be advantageous to develop a locus of control scale concerned only with work and career-related behaviors. The WSI is still in the experimental stages at this point, but results of early testing with a group of high school students seem promising. In a true experimental design study of locus of control change techniques, as hypothesized, the group receiving locus of control/career maturity change technique treatments was found to be more internal on locus of control after treatment than the control group as measured by the Work Situations Inventory. Internal consistency was found to be .74. This is considered to be more than adequate when viewed in the context of the small sample (N = 48) and the small number of items on the scale (10 items). Moreover, the scale was found to correlate significantly with the DSI, as predicted (r = .56). Thus, this experimental measure of locus of control, designed to be used in work-related studies, appears to have good evidence of reliability and concurrent and construct validity.

In summary, the Different Situations Inventory has strong evidence of excellent criterion-related, content, and construct validity coupled with good reliability. The Career Maturity Inventory appears an instrument of excellent reliability and validity. The Work Situations Inventory shows promise as a good screening device. Copies of the Different Situations Inventory and the Work Situations Inventory are on pages 197 through 199. Interested researchers can receive permission to use these instruments free of charge (except printing) by writing the senior author.

Career Maturity and Locus of Control: Selected Findings

As mentioned in Chapter 4, the juxtaposition of the two theoretical notions of how people respond to their environment and how these learned responses affect career behavior appears to offer teachers, human resource personnel, and researchers a fertile field for intervention and model building. How they do these constructs relate when tested in the field? Table V reports the findings of some recent investigations in which locus of control consistently was found to be significantly correlated with the subtests of career maturity (Crites, 1973). Populations studied ranged from Nigerian college students in the USA to junior high school students. In each instance, as one would expect, the correlations were low but significant. These findings suggest that further research, using a locus of control scale designed to measure samplings of behaviors related only to work

TABLE V
Pearson Product Moment Coefficients of Correlation on
Locus of Control versus Career Maturity

Locus of Control DSI[a]	Career Maturity CMI[b]	*r*	*p*	Population of Study	Reference
Self Report	Competence Test Part 3 Choosing a Job	.32	.004	Junior College Women *N* = 69	Cowan 1979 p.58
Self Report	Competence Test Part 4 Looking Ahead	.06	ns	Junior College Women *N* = 69	Cowan 1979 p. 58
Self Report	Competence Test Part 3 Choosing a Job	.21	.05	Compensatory College Freshmen *N* = 74	Curry 1980
Self Report	Competence Test Part 4 Looking Ahead	.19	.05	Compensatory College Freshmen *N* = 74	Curry 1980
Self Report	Competence Test Part 5 What should they do?	.30	.01	Compensatory College Freshmen *N* = 74	Curry 1980
Self Report	Competence Test Part 5 What should they do?	.26	.05	High School Students (10-12) *N* = 38	Grossman 1979 p. 81
Self Report	Attitude Scale	.49	.01	Nigerian College Students in USA *N* = 40	Ifenwanta 1978 p.48
Self Report	Competence Test Part 2 Knowing About Jobs	.33	.01	High School Seniors *N* = 50	Bigelow in review
Self Report	Competence Test Part 2 Knowing About Jobs	.31	.01	High School Seniors *N* = 75	Bigelow, 1981
Self Report	Competence Test Part 2 Knowing About Jobs	.33	.01	High School Seniors *N* = 50	Bigelow in review
Self Report	Attitude Scale	.38	.01	Disadvantaged *N* = 37 Adults	Dwyer

Note: With one exception, all correlations were significant at the .05 level or beyond. The range of the ten significant correlations with various subtests of the CMI was .19 to .49; average correlations equals .31.

[a]The Different Situatons Inventory (DSI) by Gardner & Warren (1978) was used to measure locus of control

[b]The Career Maturity Inventory (CMI) by Crites (1973) was used to measure career maturity.

TABLE VI
Pearson Product Moment Coefficients of Correlation on Locus of Control versus Career Maturity

Locus of Control DSI[a]	Career Maturity CMI[b]	*r*	*p*	Population of Study	Reference
Rater Form	Attitude Scale	.23	.001	Junior High School Students *N* = 182	Wilton 1978 p. 34
Rater Form	Competence Test Part 1 Knowing Yourself	.42	.001	Junior High School Students *N* = 182	Wilton 1978 p. 34
Rater Form	Competence Test Part 2 Knowing About Jobs	.36	.001	Junior High School Students *N* = 182	Wilton 1978 p. 34
Rater Form	Competence Test Part 3 Choosing a Job	.35	.001	Junior High School Students *N* = 182	Wilton 1978 p. 34
Rater Form	Competence Test Part 4 Looking Ahead	.25	.001	Junior High School Students *N* = 182	Wilton 1978 p. 34
Rater Form	Competence Test Part 3 Choosing a Job	.26	.01	Junior College Women *N* = 69	Cowan 1979 p. 58
Rater Form	Competence Test Part 4 Looking Ahead	.35	.002	Junior College Women *N* = 69	Cowan 1979 p. 58

NOTE: All correlations were significant at the .05 level or beyond. The range of the seven correlations with various subtests of the CMI was .23 to .42; average correlation equals .32.

[a]The Different Situations Inventory (DSI) by Gardner & Warren (1978) was used to measure locus of control.
[b]The Career Maturity Inventory (CMI) by Crites (1973) was used to measure career maturity.

and careers might offer a fruitful path for further investigation. The DSI, like most other locus of control measures, samples behaviors across a wide range of social life. Locus of control scales, including the DSI, are additive scales (Phares, 1976); that is,

> the items represent an attempt to sample I-E beliefs across a range of situations, such as interpersonal situations, school, government, work, and politics. Because [they sample] a variety of areas, [these scales] can more clearly lay claim to being measure(s) of *generalized* expectancy. (Phares, 1976, p. 42)

Thus, it would appear advantageous for teachers, human resource personnel, and counselors to develop and work with "situation-specific" scales, such as the WSI, which measure locus of control as related to job performance, career choice, etc. (see Phares, 1976). Obviously, a great deal of study needs to be done in this area if research on these two variables is to be optimized.

REFERENCES

Arrangio, J. The effects of individual goal-setting conferences and classroom instruction in human relations on locus of control, school attendance and alienation of disadvantaged high school students. Unpublished doctoral dissertation, Boston University, 1980.

Beatty, G.J. & Gardner, D.C. Goal setting and resume writing as a locus of control change technique with college women. *College Student Journal, 13(1)*:315-318, 1979.

Bigelow, E.A. The effects of consumer education and decision-making skill instruction on locus of control orientation and career maturity of high school seniors. Unpublished doctoral dissertation, Boston University, 1981.

Bigelow, E.A. Locus of control, career maturity and economic understanding. in review.

Cowan, G.J. The effects of teaching goal-setting procedures on the career maturity and classroom performance of business college women differing in locus of control. Unpublished doctoral dissertation, Boston University, 1979.

Crites, J.O. *Theory and Research Handbook for the Career Maturity Inventory.* Monterey, CA: CTB/McGraw-Hill, 1973.

Curry, J.A. The effects of life planning instruction and career counseling on locus of control orientation and career maturity scores of university compensatory education students. Unpublished doctoral dissertation, Boston University, 1980.

Dwyer, K. The effects of decision-making and life planning instruction on locus of control orientation, career maturity, and self-concept of disadvantaged adults. Unpublished doctoral dissertation, Boston University, 1981.

Gardner, D.C. Career maturity and locus of control: Important factors in career training. *College Student Journal, 15(3)*:239-246, Fall, 1981.

Gardner, D.C. Goal setting, locus of control, and work performance of mentally retarded adults. Unpublished doctoral dissertation, Boston University, 1974.

Gardner, D.C. & Beatty, G.J. Locus of control change techniques: Important variables in work training. *Education (3)*:237-242, Spring, 1980a.

Gardner, D.C. & Beatty, G.J. Personality characteristics and learning styles of disadvantaged youth: Important considerations in teaching job related language and developing work attitudes. Paper presented at the Leadership Training Institute on CETA/Vocational Education, Special Education and Vocational Rehabilitation Linkages. Hartford, CT: Sheraton-Hartford Hotel, May 4-6, 1980b.

Gardner, D.C., Beatty, G.J. & Bigelow, E.A. An evaluation of a career development seminar for high school students. In review.

Gardner, D.C., Beatty, G.J. & Bigelow, E.A. Locus of control and career maturity: A pilot evaluation of a life-planning and career development program for high school students. *Adolescence,* 1981.

Gardner, D.C. & Gardner, P.L. Goal-setting and learning in the high school resource room. *Adolescence, 18(51):* 489-493, 1974.

Gardner, D.C. & Gardner, P.L. Locus of control as related to learning effectiveness. *Reading Improvement, 11(2):* 41-42, 1974.

Gardner, D.C. & Warren, S.A. *Careers and Disabilities: A Career Education Approach.* Stamford, CT: Greylock Pub., 1978.

Hoyt, K.B. *An Introduction to Career Education.* U.S. Department of Health, Education, and Welfare Publication No. (OE) 75-00504. Washington, D.C.: U.S. Govt. Print. Office, 1975.

Hoyt, K.B., Evans, R.N., Mackin, E.F. Mangum, G.L. *Career Education: What It Is and How to Do It.* Salt Lake City, UT: Olympus, 1974.

Kliebhan, J.M. Effects of goal-setting and modeling on job performance of retarded adolescents. *American Journal of Mental Deficiency, 72:* 220-260, 1967.

Lefcourt, H.M. Internal vs. external control of reinforcement: A review. *Psychological Bulletin, 66(4):* 206-220, 1966.

Rotter, J.B. Generalized expectancies for internal versus external control of reinforcement. *Psychological Monographs,* 80 (1, whole No. 609), 1966.

Rotter, J.B. *Social Learning and Clinical Psychology.* Englewood Cliffs, NJ: Prentice-Hall, 1954.

Rotter, J.B. Some problems and misconceptions related to the construction of internal vs. external control of reinforcement. *Journal of Consulting and Clinical Psychology, 43(1):* 56-67, 1975.

Super, D.E. A theory of vocational development. *American Psychologist, 8(4):* 185-190, 1953.

Tseng, M.S. Locus of control as a determinant of job proficiency, employability, and training satisfaction of vocational rehabilitation clients. *Journal of Counseling Psychology, 17(6):* 487-491, 1970.

von Esch, P. An inquiry into the effects of a syncretic application of locus of control change techniques to a manpower training program for the economically disadvantaged. Unpublished doctoral dissertation, Boston University, 1978.

Warner, D.A. & De Jung, J.E. *Goal Setting Behavior as an Independent Variable Related to the Performance of Educable Mentally Retarded Male Adolescents on Educational Tasks of Varying Difficulty: Final Report.* U.S. Dept. of Health, Education, and Welfare, Project No. 7-1-115. Washington, D.C..: U.S. Govt. Print. Office, 1969.

APPENDIX B

DIFFERENT SITUATIONS INVENTORY AND WORK SITUATIONS INVENTORY

DIFFERENT SITUATIONS INVENTORY (D-S-I SELF)

Name (or I.D.) ______________________ Date ____________

Please consider your observations of your own behavior in the past and indicate how you think you would respond in the different situations described below. Even though both alternatives may seem appropriate to you, please choose the one you think most fitting for you. If you are not certain, please guess.

CIRCLE EITHER **A** OR **B** BUT NOT BOTH

1. In buying new shoes, I would be more influenced by:
   A. Current fashions.
   B. Personal preferences.
2. If I received an unexpected bonus, I might say:
   A. "This is my lucky day!"
   B. "Hard work pays off!"
3. After doing a very good job, I would feel:
   A. Proud that it was such good work.
   B. Proud that someone praised the work.
4. I tend to believe that an ideal future career depends most on:
   A. Hard work toward the goal, more than luck.
   B. Good luck along with the work.
5. Asked to volunteer for a community service job, I would want to know:
   A. How much time and effort would be required.
   B. If significant peers had already agreed to help.
6. When confronted by another person's disagreement, I would
   A. Withdraw gracefully.
   B. Try to clarify the issue.
7. Given a complex task, I would probably:
   A. Try to complete the task without help.
   B. Seek consultation at each stage.
8. If asked to estimate time required to bicycle five kilometers, I would:
   A. Tend to approximate the estimates of peers.
   B. Hold to own estimate even if it differs from those of peers.
9. My reaction to learning that a radio just purchased had poor tone:
   A. "That clerk sold me a bill of goods!"
   B. "Next time I'll know not to buy the cheapest one!"
10. I would prefer a TV detective show in which:
   A. The hero works alone.

B. The police consult a famous detective.

11. After failure on a test, I might attribute blame to:
    A. The test itself.
    B. Lack of preparation.
12. When somebody gets angry at me, I might feel:
    A. Maybe he'll get over it after a while.
    B. A nice letter of explanation might clear the air.
13. I might attribute difficulty in learning to improve at tennis to:
    A. Poor teaching by the coach.
    B. Not enough practice.
14. In studying for an exam, I would prefer
    A. Studying with another student.
    B. Studying in private.
15. If another person says critical things about me, my most likely reaction might be to think:
    A. "I wonder if others think the same thing about me."
    B. "Well, I'm not so sure I agree with that opinion."
16. Type of game I prefer:
    A. A game of chance.
    B. A game of skill.
17. I would feel that to reach my goal in my life, it's important to know:
    A. The right people.
    B. What I really want from life.
18. When people are mean to me, I might feel:
    A. Very concerned because it is important to have lots of friends.
    B. Very concerned, but that it is possible to get along without such people.
19. In a baseball game, I might attribute my excellent performance to:
    A. Having "a good day."
    B. Rigorous practice.
20. Not finding a personal item in an expected place, I might say:
    A. "I wonder if I left it somewhere else?"
    B. "I wonder if somebody took it by mistake?"

WORK SITUATIONS INVENTORY

Directions: Below are listed ten work situations. Please consider your own behavior in the past and indicate how you think you would respond in these situations at the present time. Even though both choices may seem right to you depending on the situation, please choose the **one** answer which you would pick most often.

1. If someone on the job got angry with me, I might say to myself:
    A. "I'll invite that person to lunch to talk it over."
    B. "I didn't do anything."
2. For people to reach their career goals, I believe that it is important for them to know:
    A. The people who can help them the most.
    B. What they really want to do in life.
3. My first feeling after doing a great job would be:

   A. To feel proud of the accomplishment.
   B. To wonder if my boss will like it.
4. If I were asked to serve on committee, the first thing I would do is.
   A. Ask what I would have to do and how long it would take.
   B. Find out if important people are on the committee.
5. If another employee makes negative statements about my work, I would most likely feel:
   A. My own opinion about the quality of the work is what really counts.
   B. Worried that other people might feel the same way.
6. If I have to turn in a report right away and I can't find it, my first thought would be:
   A. "Where did I put that report?"
   B. "Who took it?"
7. I have always believed that job success means:
   A. Knowing the right people and good luck.
   B. Hard work.
8. This morning the boss surprised me by calling me into the office and giving me a raise. My first thought was.
   A. "I deserved every penny of it."
   B. "Wow, am I lucky!"
9. When a fellow employee doesn't like me, I might say to myself:
   A. "I need to find another way to deal with that person."
   B. "Just my luck to be in this department."
10. If my work is faster and better than everyone else's, I would:
   A. Slow down a little.
   B. Ask the boss for a raise.

INDEX